CHRISTMAS COOKIES AND CANDIES

Also by Barbara Myers

Great Dinner Parties
Woman's Day Old-Fashioned Desserts

CHRISTMAS COOKIES AND CANDIES

BARBARA MYERS

Rawson, Wade Publishers, Inc.
New York

Library of Congress Cataloging in Publication Data

Myers, Barbara.
Christmas cookies and candies

Includes index.
1. Cookies.   2. Confectionery.   3. Christmas
cookery.   I. Title.
TX772.M9   1979   641.8′654   79–64204
ISBN 0–89256–107–6

Designed by Gloria Gentile

To Hedwig Mueller—*ein Mensch der dich begeistert*

CONTENTS

CHRISTMAS
COOKIES
AND
CANDIES

ꟼNTRODUCTION

The baking and giving of Christmas cookies is an age-old custom in countries around the world where the holiday is celebrated. In America we honor this tradition, and include homemade candies as well, as a part of the warm, outgoing spirit that we all share during the holiday season.

This special collection of traditional cookie and candy recipes comes from nearly a dozen and a half countries. Our greatest sources of Christmas cookies are North and Central Europe—particularly Germany, the Scandinavian countries, and the Netherlands—where the baking of Christmas cookies has long been considered an art. The candies, however, are mostly old-fashioned American favorites that have persisted through our brief history and represent only a short step back in time as compared to the Old World cookies.

Our immigrant ancestors brought with them many cherished cookie recipes from the old countries. When they settled in the various parts of the United States, they preserved these old traditions. Consequently, many of the cookies we make today show the Old World influence of these settlers. Most of the recipes included here are close to the original concepts, changed only to adapt to modern measurements and baking techniques. Others originated here, such as ice-box cookies, certain drop and bar cookies, and our own white Christmas cut-outs, which are gaily frosted and decorated.

Where possible the foreign names of the recipes have been retained as a source of identification and to provide a sense of the past.

Among the cookie specialties are crisp rolled cookies, sometimes cut simply, sometimes defined with special cutters. Others are put through a press or hand-shaped into traditional holiday symbols. There are drop cookies, bars and squares, and dainty wafers. And there are delicate meringue kisses and chewy macaroons.

Some are filled with fruits and nuts; others are flavored with butter, ground nuts, or spices.

Some cookies are glazed with a simple frosting, or decorated with colorful candied fruits, sugars, or other decorations. Others are given a snowy appearance by being rolled in powdered sugar.

The Christmas candies are cut or formed into simple shapes that need no decoration. Their appeal lies in their special textures and intriguing flavors.

Flavors vary, from vanilla to caramel, but chocolate is dominant because it is a special American favorite.

There are creamy candies, delightfully chewy ones, and crunchy or hard varieties—and the dried fruit-and-nut confections often called "sugarplums."

A gift assortment of delicious cookies or candies, or a platter heaped with holiday creations when friends or relatives drop in, suggests a special warm-hearted way of saying, "Merry Christmas."

ꟼNGREDIENTS

The information given below applies to both cookies and candies.

Butter: Frequently, Old World recipes for cookies call for sweet butter. This is unsalted butter, which many cookie bakers believe has a fresher flavor than the more familiar lightly salted butter. This is true if the butter is very fresh, since salt is used primarily as a preservative. Salted butter may be substituted, but if the recipe contains salt, the amount should be adjusted. Although many of the recipes requiring sweet butter do not call for salt, the substitution of salted butter will not alter the flavor greatly and may enhance it to adjust to modern-day American palates. Margarine or hydrogenated shortening, both of which are lacking in flavor, are not satisfactory substitutes when a basic butter flavor is essential.

Sugar: In general, granulated sugar is required. If the sugar is lumpy, crush it or strain it to remove the large particles, which are difficult to blend in or dissolve. This is an important consideration in the prevention of crystalization in the making of candies.

Some recipes call for fine granulated sugar. It may be purchased (often labeled "superfine") or it can be prepared by whirling granulated sugar in a food processor until a fine consistency is reached.

Brown Sugar: Light or dark brown sugar can be used interchangeably in the recipes. The choice is a matter of taste. Light brown sugar has a milder flavor and is preferred for most candies; old-fashioned dark brown sugar is often preferred for cookies. If lumpy, press through a wire sieve before using.

Confectioners' Sugar: This powdered sugar is used

primarily for glazes and frostings on cookies. If very hot or boiling water is used, it is not necessary to sift the sugar before using; it will not dissolve properly in cold water without having been sifted. Sifted confectioners' sugar is necessary for coating or dusting baked cookies. For dusting, put the unsifted sugar in a wire strainer and shake lightly over the cookies.

Pearl Sugar: This type of sugar is used for decorating. It is imported from Sweden or Germany, and can be found in certain specialty shops that sell Scandinavian or German products. The granules are coarse and irregular. Crushed loaf sugar (sugar cubes) makes the best substitute; granulated sugar is too fine. Spread the sugar tablets on a board, cover with a sheet of waxed paper, then pound lightly. The mixture will crush unevenly, so the pearl sugar (or crystal sugar, as it is often called) is preferred.

Chocolate: The type of chocolate used is specified in the recipes.

To melt chocolate: Place the chocolate in a double boiler set over simmering water. When the chocolate softens and begins to melt, remove the pan from the water and stir the chocolate until it is smooth. It should be cooled slightly before using.

Kirsch (or Kirschwasser): This is a clear cherry brandy used in some German and Swiss recipes. It is used not only for flavor but also as a leavening agent. Many German cookie recipes call for white rum with satisfying results.

Spices: All spices called for are ground spices unless otherwise specified. Most are easily obtained. Cardamom may be purchased in Scandinavian and Indian specialty shops. If only whole cardamom (whitish pods) is available, discard the papery outer shell, then grind the black seeds to powder with a mortar and pestle.

Nuts, Dried and Candied Fruits: Some measurements for these ingredients are given by weight rather than by the cup, for greater accuracy. The following approximations will be helpful if you do not own a scale.

Note: All measurements for nuts (in the recipes and as listed below) are for shelled nuts.

1 pound almonds = 3 cups
1 pound hazelnuts = 3¼ cups
1 pound pecans = 4¼ cups
1 pound walnuts = 4¼ cups
1 pound raisins = 3 cups
1 pound pitted dates = 2 cups
1 pound cut candied fruit or peels = 3 cups

To blanch almonds or pistachios: Cover the nuts with boiling water. Let them stand for 3 minutes, then drain them. Slip off the skins by pinching them with your fingers. Spread the nuts out and let them dry overnight; or dry the nuts in a 200° oven for about 30 minutes, then let them cool.

To split almonds: Blanch as described above. As soon as the almonds can be handled, split them in half with the tip of a knife. If blanched almonds have been purchased, cover them with boiling water and let them stand until they are slightly softened.

Note: Sliced or slivered almonds are difficult to prepare; they should be purchased.

To toast almonds: Place whole blanched almonds in one layer in a dry, heavy skillet. Stir over low heat until they turn color. Do not over-brown them because they continue to darken as they cool.

To grind nuts: Many of the cookie recipes call for ground nuts as a replacement for part of the flour required. When they are ground, nuts should be light and fluffy. They must be dry before grinding. (See above: To blanch almonds or pistachios.)

Use a nut grinder, a food processor, or a blender. A meat grinder will turn them oily. A nut grinder or food processor is easier to use: a blender takes longer because only a half cup can be blended at one time.

When grinding nuts in a food processor, watch carefully because they will quickly become pasty. Perfect results can be obtained if the ground nuts can be mixed with sugar or flour when preparing the cookie dough (check individual recipes). Use the following method:

Process up to 2 cups of nuts until they are coarsely chopped; then add part of the flour or sugar (including confectioners' sugar) and continue processing until the mixture is smooth.

CHRISTMAS COOKIES

BAKING AND STORING

The baking of Christmas cookies should be considered an artistic endeavor. Great care must be taken during the mixing, forming, and baking so that the results approach perfection.

The recipes and guidelines which follow will help.

Helpful Tips

1. Most cookies require a short baking time, so an accurate oven temperature is important to assure proper baking. If you are unsure of the oven thermostat, purchase an oven thermometer (the mercury type is best). If your oven is off a few degrees, adjust the thermostat accordingly when setting the oven temperature for baking.

Note: All of the cookies presented here should be baked in a preheated oven. Allow 10 to 15 minutes to heat to the proper temperature.

2. Cookies must be baked evenly or the results will be less than perfect.

Pans should be heavy so that the cookies do not brown on the bottom before they are done. Pans must not be so large that the heat cannot circulate freely; there must be at least 2 inches between the edges of the pan and the sides of the oven.

Cookies will bake more evenly if only one sheet is baked at a time. The rack should be placed in the middle of the oven so that the heat is equally distributed.

If it is necessary to bake two sheets at one time, a rotation method should be used. Place one rack in the upper third of the oven and the second in the lower third. Set the first sheet of cookies on the lower rack; when the next sheet is prepared, move the first one to the top and insert the second on the lower rack.

Some ovens have "hot spots," which will cause uneven baking. If this is a problem, reverse the sheet about halfway through the baking.

Cookies should be cut, formed, or dropped to turn out approximately the same size, so that they will be done at the same time.

Baking too many cookies at a time on one sheet will also cause uneven baking. They should be separated as directed in the recipes, allowing extra space at the edge of the sheet. If the recipes do not indicate otherwise, space the cookies one inch apart.

3. If the baking pans or cookie sheets are to be greased, brush them with soft or melted sweet butter or shortening. Salted butter or oil may cause the cookies to stick.

If the pans are to be greased and floured, grease lightly and sprinkle a little flour in the pan; then shake it to produce an even coating. Invert the pan (over the sink) and rap on it to remove the excess flour. Too much flour will make the cookies pasty on the bottom.

4. In the absence of other instructions, cookies should be removed from the cookie sheet while they are hot and placed on racks for cooling. This will prevent them from sweating and becoming soggy. Allow thin or fragile cookies to cool on the pan a minute or two before removing in order to give them time to set.

If the cookies are to be cooled in the pan (or on the cookie sheet), set the pan on a rack for cooling.

5. When butter and sugar are to be creamed together, the butter will blend better if it is slightly softened. It should be allowed to stand at room temperature just long enough so that it is workable, not until it becomes so soft that it loses shape.

For a fine texture, the mixture should be creamed thoroughly. When the flour is added, the dough should be mixed just long enough to incorporate it, or the cookies will be tough.

6. Some butter cookies are made by cutting the butter into a flour-and-sugar mixture (as one does for pie crust) with a pastry blender or by using your fingertips. The butter should be cold or firm. Cut the butter into small pieces from the stick, dropping them into the mixture as you cut.

7. Although most of the cookies can be mixed with either a wooden spoon or an electric mixer, the electric mixer is essential for sponge cookies, meringues, and some macaroons.

Sponge cookies are made without shortening. Producing a fine texture requires long beating of whole eggs and sugar before the flour is added.

Meringues and macaroons require beaten egg whites and sugar. The egg whites are beaten until stiff, then the sugar is added slowly while the beating continues. After the sugar is incorporated, further beating is required until the mixture is very stiff. If the sugar is added too quickly or the mixture beaten insufficiently, it will not hold its shape.

8. For cookies that are rolled and cut, the dough must be firm and not sticky for proper rolling. Chilling is generally required. (If the dough seems excessively sticky after preparing, work in a little extra flour before chilling it.)

For soft doughs a lightly floured board or floured pastry cloth should be used. Use only as much flour as is necessary to cover the surface because excess flour will make the cookies tough. If the dough is fairly firm, it may be rolled between sheets of waxed paper. Cookies rolled this way will be more tender.

Roll out small portions at a time, keeping the remainder refrigerated so that it remains firm.

As the cookies are cut, the scraps should be set aside and re-rolled together. Cookies produced from the scraps will be less tender.

9. Most simple, hand-formed cookies can be shaped (especially if the dough is chilled) without flouring your hands. If necessary, dust your hands lightly. The fancier hand-shaped cookies are often formed by rolling a small portion of dough (again with the hands) into a strip before shaping. A plastic-topped counter is ideal; if the dough seems sticky (even after chilling), roll it out on a lightly floured board.

10. For cookies that are formed by using a cookie press, follow the manufacturer's directions for assembly and use. Cookie presses vary.

With few exceptions, the dough is pressed out directly onto an *un*greased cookie sheet so that the dough will adhere. If the sheet is warm, the dough will not stick.

The dough for these cookies is usually made and used immediately. If the dough is too soft, the designs may not be sharp, or the dough may not break off neatly when the press is lifted. If this is a problem, chill the dough briefly. If the dough is too stiff, it will be difficult to press.

11. Bar-type cookies that are baked in a large shallow pan will be extra brown and crisp around the edges. Leave them that way if you like, or trim away the brown part before cutting the remainder.

12. Drop cookies (including meringues and macaroons) are prepared by dropping the dough onto a cookie sheet from a teaspoon. A tableware teaspoon, not a measuring teaspoon, should be used unless otherwise specified. A small portion of the dough on the tip of the

spoon is eased off with a second spoon or with your finger.

Storing

All Christmas cookies, whether soft, crisp, or hard, should be thoroughly cooled, then stored in tightly covered containers. Metal cans, plastic containers, and foil-lined cardboard boxes can be used, as can plastic bags for cookies which are not fragile. Cookies should be stored in a cool, dry place.

Soft and crisp cookies should not be stored together; nor should cookies of various types, because of the mingling of flavors.

Decorated cookies (particularly those with a chocolate glaze), cookies containing sticky fruits, and fragile cookies should be stored with waxed paper between the layers. This will prevent sticking, loss of decoration, and breakage.

Soft cookies containing dried fruit, honey, molasses, or syrup, and spice cookies with a crisp texture keep best. In fact, many of these cookies need to be stored for several weeks to "ripen" in both texture and flavor. They continue to improve with age.

Note: If soft cookies dry or crisp ones become too hard during storage, half an apple or a slice of bread will restore the moisture. Place on a sheet of waxed paper on top of the cookies, and replace the apple or bread as necessary.

Cookies rich with butter vary in texture and keeping qualities. Those that are especially delicate and tender will keep only a week to 10 days when stored at a cool room temperature. Kept longer, they lose the fresh flavor for which they are prized.

Crisp butter cookies and some that contain ground

nuts will keep for weeks with proper storage. But they will gradually lose flavor and eventually may become rancid.

Meringues and macaroons, which are made with whipped egg whites, have varying keeping qualities. Those made primarily from beaten egg whites (even though filled with chopped nuts or fruits) tend to dry out rapidly. They should be stored at room temperature and kept only a week or so. Those that contain ground nuts and are slightly chewy can be kept somewhat longer.

All baked cookies freeze well for many months when placed in tightly sealed containers. Since most cookies keep well at room temperature, freezing is suggested only for those that have a short storage life. Of course, if you are baking far in advance of the holidays, freezing may be necessary.

When removing the cookies from the freezer for thawing, let the container stand several hours at room temperature before opening it. This prevents moisture from collecting on the baked cookies.

If crisp cookies (unglazed) seem less than crisp, place them on a cookie sheet and heat in a 300° oven for a few minutes.

ROLLED COOKIES

The cookies described in this section are shaped with a knife, a pastry wheel, or a simple round cutter. They include several Old World favorites, such as spicy German Pfeffernusse, or Peppernuts; Ischler Tortchen, the Austrian sandwich cookie that is filled with apricot jam and glazed with chocolate; Fattigmans Bakkels, the fried Norwegian twists known as Poor Man's Cake; Vanilla Sticks, rich with almonds and iced with meringue; and Bohemian Kolacky, made with a cream cheese dough.

RUSSIAN STRIPS

A crisp, easily made cookie, also known as German Almond Bread.

> ½ *pound butter*
> 1½ *cups sugar*
> 2 *egg yolks*
> ½ *teaspoon vanilla*
> 2 *cups unsifted all-purpose flour*
> ¼ *pound unblanched almonds, ground*
> 1 *egg white, slightly beaten*
> *Red- and green-colored sugars*
> *Tiny multicolored candies*

Cream the butter with the sugar until light. Add the egg yolks and vanilla; beat until fluffy.

Gradually add the flour and almonds, a little at a time, mixing with a spoon at first, then knead well with your hands. If the dough is too soft for rolling, chill until firm enough.

Divide the dough into thirds. Roll out each portion on a lightly floured board slightly less than ¼ inch thick. Cut into 3 x 1-inch strips, using a sharp knife or pastry wheel. Place 1 inch apart on an ungreased cookie sheet.

Brush the strips with the egg white. Sprinkle each with red or green sugar, or with candies (just down the centers).

Bake in a 350° oven until golden, about 15 minutes.
Makes about 5 dozen.

VANILLA STICKS

Finger-size strips of almond dough iced with a ribbon of meringue. These are a "must" for a Christmas cookie assortment.

8 egg whites
½ teaspoon salt
1 tablespoon vanilla
2 pounds confectioners' sugar
1 to 1¼ pounds unblanched almonds, ground
Confectioners' sugar for rolling

Beat the egg whites until foamy; add the salt and continue beating until they stand in stiff peaks, adding the vanilla toward the end. Gradually add the sugar and continue beating for 15 minutes after the last of the sugar has been added. (An electric mixer is a necessity.)

Remove half the mixture to a separate smaller bowl (to be used for icing). Fold the ground almonds into the remaining mixture; blend well. (Add enough almonds to make a stiff dough which can be handled easily for rolling.)

Roll the dough about ⅛ inch thick on a board sprinkled with confectioners' sugar. Cut into 4 x ½-inch strips, using a thin sharp knife. Arrange the strips close together on a greased cookie sheet (they will not spread). Frost the tops with the reserved meringue mixture (a table knife works best here). Let dry 5 minutes before baking.

Bake in a 300° oven until the tops are just beginning to turn tan, about 15 minutes. Remove from the cookie sheet at once. When cooled, store in a tightly covered container to keep crisp.

Makes about 7 dozen sticks.

LECKERLI

A Swiss specialty made with ground hazelnuts and almonds. The cookies are cut into squares before baking and glazed when removed from the oven.

½ pound unblanched hazelnuts, ground
½ pound unblanched almonds, ground
1¾ cups sugar
4 egg whites
Grated rind of 1 orange
2 tablespoons kirsch or white rum
Flour and sugar for rolling
Glaze (recipe follows)

Combine the hazelnuts, almonds, and sugar. Add the unbeaten egg whites, orange rind, and kirsch. Mix thoroughly with your hands. Chill the dough 5 to 6 hours.

Sprinkle a board with equal portions of flour and sugar. Pat one quarter of the dough out onto the board; sprinkle a little of the flour-and-sugar mixture on the top. Roll out to slightly more than ¼-inch thickness. Cut into 1½-inch squares (or slightly less). Repeat with the remaining dough.

Arrange the cookies an inch apart on a greased and floured cookie sheet. Bake in a 325° oven for 20 minutes, or until fairly firm. (They will not brown.)

Remove the cookies from the oven and immediately brush with the Glaze. Let the cookies cool on the cookie sheet before removing.

Makes about 4½ to 5 dozen.

Note: These cookies are slightly chewy: they keep well in a covered container.

Glaze

1 cup confectioners' sugar
½ teaspoon vanilla
1 teaspoon kirsch or white rum
2 tablespoons hot water (approx.)

Combine the sugar, vanilla, kirsch, and enough hot water to make a smooth icing that will spread without running.

SAND TARTS

Also known as Saint Hearts, these rolled cookies are traditionally cut into diamond shapes and dusted with sugar and cinnamon.

> ¼ pound butter
> 1 cup sugar
> 2 egg yolks
> 1 tablespoon heavy cream
> 1 teaspoon vanilla
> 1¾ cups sifted all-purpose flour
> ¼ teaspoon salt
> ½ teaspoon baking powder
> Heavy cream for glazing
> 1 tablespoon sugar mixed with 1 teaspoon cinnamon

Cream the butter and the sugar. Gradually beat in the egg yolks, cream, and vanilla.

Sift the flour with the salt and baking powder. Add to the butter mixture; blend well. Chill, covered, at least 3 hours, or overnight.

Divide the mixture into three parts. Roll out one part at a time between sheets of waxed paper to ⅛-inch thickness. Cut in the traditional diamond shape, or use a 2½-inch round cutter. Brush the tops with cream and sprinkle with the cinnamon-sugar mixture.

Bake in a 375° oven for about 6 minutes, or until delicately browned. Let cool slightly before removing to racks for complete cooling.

Makes about 4 dozen.

FATTIGMANS BAKKELS
(Norwegian Poor Man's Cake)

A deep-fried Norwegian pastry.

>   *1 egg*
>   *2 egg yolks*
>   *½ cup sugar*
>   *¼ teaspoon salt*
>   *2 tablespoons butter, melted*
>   *2 tablespoons heavy cream*
>   *1 tablespoon orange-flavored liqueur*
>   *2 cups sifted all-purpose flour*
>   *Oil for deep-fat frying*
>   *Confectioners' sugar*

Beat the egg, egg yolks, sugar, and salt until light. Stir in the butter, cream, and orange liqueur. Add the flour, blend until smooth. (If necessary add a little more flour to make a stiff dough.)

Roll out a third of the dough at a time on a lightly floured board to about ⅛-inch thickness. Cut into 3 x 1-inch strips with a crinkle-edged pastry wheel, cutting the ends diagonally. Make a lengthwise slit in the center of each, and pull one end completely through so that the center is twisted.

Fry a few at a time in a skillet containing at least 2 inches of hot oil, heated to 350°. Fry until a delicate brown, turning once. Drain on paper towels. When cool, dust with confectioners' sugar.

Makes about 5 dozen.

Note: These fried pastries are best when freshly made.

PFEFFERNUSSE
(German Peppernuts)

German peppernuts are tiny spice cookies which contain pepper as well as several other spices. A drop of brandy on the top before baking causes them to "pop," giving them a characteristic topknot.

> *4 eggs*
> *2 cups sugar*
> *4 cups sifted all-purpose flour*
> *1 teaspoon baking powder*
> *¼ teaspoon salt*
> *¼ teaspoon pepper*
> *2 teaspoons cinnamon*
> *½ teaspoon nutmeg*
> *½ teaspoon allspice*
> *½ teaspoon cloves*
> *¼ teaspoon mace*
> *Grated rind of 1 lemon*
> *½ cup candied citron, finely chopped*
> *½ cup unblanched almonds, ground*
> *Brandy*

Beat the eggs until fluffy in an electric mixer set at medium speed. Gradually add the sugar, beating constantly. Then continue beating 15 minutes longer.

Sift the flour with the baking powder, salt, pepper, cinnamon, nutmeg, allspice, cloves, and mace. Add to the beaten egg mixture in thirds, blending thoroughly after each addition: mix the lemon rind, citron, and almonds in the last third before adding.

Turn half the dough out onto a lightly floured board.

Roll ½ inch thick. Cut with a 1-inch round cutter (the inside of a doughnut cutter works well) and place an inch apart on a greased cookie sheet. Let stand uncovered at room temperature overnight.

When ready to bake, turn the cookies over so that the moist side is up and put a drop of brandy in the center of each.

Bake in a 300° oven for 20 minutes, or until the cookies are popped and baked through. (Break one in half; if not sticky, the cookies are done.)

Makes 7½ to 8 dozen.

Note: These cookies improve with aging; store in a tightly covered container. Add a piece of apple to the container a few days before serving to soften them.

ISCHLER TORTCHEN

Tartlets from Ischler, a small town in Austria. Actually a sandwich-type cookie filled with apricot jam, iced with chocolate, and garnished with half an almond. These are aristocrats of the cookie kingdom.

> 2 cups sifted all-purpose flour
> 1 cup blanched almonds, ground
> ½ pound sweet butter (cold)
> ½ cup sugar
> ½ cup apricot jam (approx.)
> 4 ounces (4 squares) semisweet chocolate
> 1 tablespoon butter for icing
> ¼ cup blanched almond halves (approx.)

Combine the flour and ground almonds in a bowl. Slice the cold butter into the flour mixture. Work with your fingertips to coarse crumbs. Add the sugar. Then work the dough until smooth and well blended by kneading with your hands. Chill the dough if necessary. (If you use cold butter and work the dough quickly and lightly, it can be rolled without chilling.)

Roll the dough between sheets of waxed paper to slightly less than ⅛-inch thickness.

Cut into 1¾-inch rounds with a cookie cutter. Place an inch apart on an ungreased cookie sheet.

Bake in a 350° oven for 8 to 10 minutes, or until a light golden color. Let stand a few minutes to firm, then remove to racks for cooling.

When the cookies are cooled, spread half the cookies with apricot jam, then top with the remaining cookies (sandwich fashion).

Partially melt the chocolate with the 1 tablespoon of

butter; remove from heat and stir rapidly until smooth and slightly cooled. Coat the tops of the filled cookies with the chocolate, spreading thinly to the edges. (A table knife is easiest to work with.) Garnish each cookie with half an almond, rounded-side up.

When the icing is set, store the cookies between sheets of waxed paper in a tightly covered container.

Makes 4½ to 5 dozen cookies.

Note: These cookies are best when freshly made. They will keep well for a few days, then lose their crispness. For longer storage, bake and store the cookies; fill and frost them later.

POLISH POPPY SEED COOKIES

One of several Old World cookies which utilize whole spice seeds for flavor as well as for garnish.

> ½ pound sweet butter
> ¾ cup sugar
> 1 teaspoon vanilla
> 5 hard-cooked egg yolks
> 2 cups sifted all-purpose flour
> ½ teaspoon salt
> 1 egg beaten with 1 teaspoon milk
> Poppy seeds

Cream the butter with the sugar and vanilla. Press the egg yolks through a sieve into the creamed mixture; mix lightly but thoroughly.

Combine the flour and the salt; blend into the egg yolk mixture. Chill until firm enough to roll.

Roll out small portions at a time onto a lightly floured board to ¼-inch thickness. Cut into simple rounds with a 1¾- to 2-inch cutter.

Space an inch apart on a cookie sheet. Brush with the egg-and-milk mixture; then sprinkle the tops with poppy seeds.

Bake in a 350° oven for 10 minutes, or until golden.
Makes about 3 dozen.

BOHEMIAN KOLACKY

A Czechoslovakian cookie made from a rich cream-cheese dough.

> ½ *pound butter*
> 3 *packages (9 ounces) cream cheese*
> 2 *cups sifted all-purpose flour*
> 2 *tablespoons sugar*
> ½ *teaspoon salt*
> 2 *teaspoons baking powder*
> 2 *medium-size eggs, well beaten*
>   *Cherry or apricot jam*

Cream the butter and cheese until well blended.

Sift the flour with the sugar, salt, and baking powder. Work into the creamed mixture, then add the beaten eggs, mixing to form a stiff dough. Chill until firm enough for rolling, several hours or overnight.

Roll out one quarter of the dough at a time on a lightly floured board to slightly less than ¼-inch thickness. (Keep the remainder chilled.) Cut into rounds with a 1¾-inch cutter. Make a deep indentation in the center of each with your thumb. Fill the depression with jam. (An excess amount will bubble up and spill onto the pastry while it bakes and spoil the appearance.) Place on an ungreased cookie sheet, spacing the cookies an inch apart.

Bake in a 375° oven for about 15 minutes, or until golden.

Makes 5 to 5½ dozen.

COOKIE CUT-OUTS

All of these Christmas cookies are made from rolled dough cut into interesting shapes. Some require the observance of European traditions which call for special cutters—stars, rosettes, and crescents—and a specified method of decorating. The most famous of these is the German Springerle, which calls for a carved board or rolling pin that produces raised designs on the finished rectangular cakes. For others, the choice of shapes is limited only by the cutters at hand, and the finishing touches are limited only by one's own creative spirit.

Among the European treasures are Swedish Pepparkakor, a cut-out spice cookie with edges defined by a ribbon of ornamental frosting; Honey Lebkuchen from Germany, with a decoration of almonds and citron and an attractive crackled glaze; and Zimtsterne, another German favorite intriguingly scented with cinnamon and shaped like stars. Also included are: American Christmas Cookie Cut-Outs, which are white sugar cookies, gaily frosted and decorated; and Gingerbread Men, the favorite of children everywhere.

CHRISTMAS COOKIE CUT-OUTS

America's traditional Christmas cookies are shaped with fancy cutters. Although there are dozens of recipes for the basic dough, which is made with butter and without spices, the one presented here is among the easiest and the best. The cookie shapes are limited only by the number of cutters at hand; the icings and decorations are limited only by one's imagination.

> ½ pound butter
> ½ cup sugar
> 1 egg
> 2 teaspoons vanilla
> 3 cups sifted all-purpose flour
> ½ teaspoon baking powder
> ⅛ teaspoon salt
>   Sugar Glaze (recipe follows)
>   Colored sugars, tiny multicolored candies, and silver dragees

Cream the butter and sugar together until fluffy. Beat in the egg and vanilla.

Sift together the flour, baking powder, and salt. Stir into the butter mixture, blend well. Chill thoroughly.

Roll out small portions of the dough at one time to slightly less than ⅛-inch thickness. Cut with Christmas cookie cutters. Place an inch apart on a lightly greased cookie sheet.

Bake at 350° for 10 to 12 minutes, or until delicately browned at the edges. Remove to a rack to cool.

Frost the cookies with the Sugar Glaze, using a knife for spreading. Before the glaze hardens, sprinkle with decorations as desired.

Makes about 5 dozen cut-outs.

Sugar Glaze

1½ cups sifted confectioners' sugar
3 tablespoons light corn syrup
2 tablespoons milk
¼ teaspoon vanilla
Food coloring (optional)

Combine the sugar, corn syrup, milk, and vanilla; blend well. Tint portions of the frosting with food coloring if desired.

Cover with a damp cloth until ready to use.

PEPPARKAKOR
(Swedish Ginger Cookies)

The Scandinavian versions of these crisp spice cookies vary in shape and decoration. The Norwegians cut the dough into diamonds and place an almond in the center. The Danes cut them into simple rounds with an identical garnish. The Swedes, however, prefer more fanciful shapes, such as hearts, stars, roosters, or reindeer. The various shapes are decorated by lining the edges with fine ribbons of ornamental white frosting, put on in straight lines, zigzags, whirled loops, or dots.

¼ pound butter
¾ cup sugar
1 small egg
1 tablespoon light molasses
Juice (2 tablespoons) and grated rind of ½ orange
2½ cups sifted all-purpose flour
1 teaspoon baking soda
1½ teaspoons ginger
1½ teaspoons cinnamon
½ teaspoon cloves
Royal Icing (recipe follows)

Cream the butter with the sugar. Add the egg and beat until fluffy. Stir in the molasses, orange juice, and rind; mix well.

Sift together the flour, baking soda, ginger, cinnamon, and cloves. Add to the creamed mixture, stirring until blended. Chill the dough thoroughly.

Roll out small portions of the dough at a time on a lightly floured board to slightly less than ⅛-inch thickness.

Cut into desired shapes with fancy cookie cutters.

Place 1 inch apart on a lightly greased cookie sheet. Bake in a 375° oven for 8 to 10 minutes, or until the color deepens to a golden brown. (Watch carefully toward the end of baking; this happens quickly.) Remove from cookie sheets immediately and cool on racks.

When cool, outline the cookie shapes with Royal Icing, using straight or zigzag lines, swirled loops or dots. (Use a decorating tube with a 1/16-inch opening; or make a cone by folding and rolling heavy paper; tape it together and snip off the tip to make a 1/16-inch opening.)

Makes about 5 dozen.

Royal Icing

> 1 egg white
> Dash of salt
> ¼ teaspoon cream of tartar
> ¼ teaspoon vanilla
> 1¼ cups sifted confectioners' sugar (approx.)

Beat the egg white, salt, and cream of tartar until stiff peaks form (use an electric mixer). Add the vanilla; then gradually beat in just enough confectioners' sugar so that the icing is stiff but still thin enough to push through a 1/16-inch opening of a decorating tube tip.

Cover with a damp cloth until ready to use.

EIER KRINGEL
(German Egg Yolk Cookies)

Numerous German cookies which are made with egg yolks are known by this name. These recipes utilize the yolks left from such traditional favorites as Zimtsterne (Cinnamon Stars) and Vanilla Sticks, and numerous other cookies that call for egg whites.

> 2 hard-cooked egg yolks
> 2 raw egg yolks
> ¼ pound butter
> ½ cup sugar
> 2 cups sifted cake flour
> ½ teaspoon cardamom
> 1 teaspoon grated lemon rind
> 1 egg white, slightly beaten
> ¼ cup sugar mixed with ½ cup chopped
>   blanched almonds

Put the hard-cooked egg yolks through a wire sieve. (To do this easily, press them through with your fingers.) Add the raw egg yolks; mix well.

Cream the butter and sugar; add to the egg yolks and mix thoroughly. Stir in the flour, cardamom, and lemon rind; blend well. Chill for 1 hour.

Roll out small portions of the dough at a time on a lightly floured board to ⅛-inch thickness. Cut with a 2½-inch doughnut cutter. Brush with the egg white, then sprinkle the tops with the sugar-and-almond mixture. Place on an ungreased cookie sheet.

Bake in a 375° oven for about 10 minutes, or until delicately browned.

Makes about 4 dozen.

HONEY LEBKUCHEN

Though they originated in Germany, Lebkuchen appear in some version in most northern European countries. Sometimes they are made like cakes; sometimes they are brittle cookies. This German version is made with honey and turns out soft and chewy. The dough is prepared several days before baking to let the spices mellow. At baking time, the rolled dough is cut into simple shapes and decorated with citron and almonds. As soon as they come from the oven, the cookies are brushed with a glaze that (upon drying) produces an attractive crackled effect.

⅔ cup honey
1½ cups sugar
¼ pound butter
6 cups sifted all-purpose flour
½ teaspoon salt
1½ teaspoons baking soda
1½ teaspoons cloves
½ teaspoon cardamom
Grated rind of 1 lemon
½ cup candied citron, finely chopped
1 cup blanched almonds, finely chopped
2 small eggs
Blanched almond halves and citron for decorating
White Sugar Glaze (recipe follows)

Heat the honey in a saucepan until thin and slightly darkened. Add the sugar and butter; stir until melted, then remove from the heat. Pour the mixture into a mixing bowl and cool to lukewarm. (Do not allow it to become stiff.)

Sift 2 cups of the flour with the salt, baking soda, cloves, and cardamom. Mix in the lemon rind, citron, and almonds. Stir into the slightly cooled honey mixture.

Break the eggs into a measuring cup and add enough cold water to make ¾ cup liquid; beat until blended. Add to the honey mixture alternately with the remaining flour. Cover the bowl and let stand in a cool place (do not refrigerate) for 3 to 4 days. (This aging improves the flavor.)

Roll out small portions of the dough on a lightly floured board slightly thicker than ⅛ inch.

Hearts: Cut the rolled dough with a heart-shaped cookie cutter, about 2½ inches in size. Press an almond lightly into the center and encircle it with small pieces of citron.

Rounds: Cut with a 3-inch round cutter. Press 5 almond halves (rounded-side up) around the edge with the small ends pointing toward the center, and place a piece of citron in the middle.

Oblongs: Cut with a knife into 2½ x 2-inch rectangles. Place two almonds in the center and decorate the corners with citron.

Place the decorated cookies on a lightly greased cookie sheet, spacing them an inch apart. Bake one sheet at a time in a 350° oven for 6 to 8 minutes, or until golden brown but still slightly soft.

Immediately transfer the cookies to a cooling rack. Brush the hot cookies with the White Sugar Glaze. When the cookies are cool and the glaze has hardened, store in a tightly covered container.

Makes about 8 dozen.

Note: These cookies can be baked several weeks in advance. They may be eaten immediately but improve with age.

White Sugar Glaze

1 tablespoon lemon juice
6 to 8 tablespoons hot milk
1 pound unsifted confectioners' sugar

Stir the lemon juice and enough hot milk into the confectioners' sugar to make a smooth icing that will spread without running. (Use a pastry brush for spreading on the cookies.)

GINGERBREAD MEN

One for the children. The dough is easy to roll, fun to cut and decorate.

¾ cup dark corn syrup
½ pound butter
1 cup sugar
1 tablespoon vinegar
1 egg
5 cups sifted all-purpose flour
1½ teaspoons baking soda
1 teaspoon ginger
1 teaspoon cinnamon
¼ teaspoon salt
Confectioners' Sugar Icing (recipe follows)
Raisins

Heat the corn syrup in a small saucepan. When it comes to a boil, pour over the butter and sugar, which have been placed in a mixing bowl. Add the vinegar and stir until smooth; cool.

Blend in the egg. Sift the flour, baking soda, ginger, cinnamon, and salt together. Then sift again into the corn syrup mixture; mix well. Cover and chill overnight.

Remove about ¾ cup of the dough at a time (to make one gingerbread man). Roll out on a lightly floured board into a rectangle approximately 8 x 5 inches. Cut with a large (7 to 8 inch) gingerbread-man cutter.

Place an inch apart on a greased cookie sheet. Bake at 350° for 10 to 12 minutes, or until the cookies are an even golden brown. (Watch carefully.) Cool slightly, then remove from the cookie sheet to cooling racks.

When completely cool, frost with Confectioners' Sugar Icing. Before it sets, press raisins into the glaze to represent eyes, nose, mouth, and buttons.

Makes 15 to 18 figures.

Note: These gingerbread men are frosted and decorated simply. For more elaborate versions, the frosting may be colored as desired and a variety of decorations used.

Confectioners' Sugar Icing

1 cup confectioners' sugar
1 teaspoon butter
1 teaspoon vanilla
1 tablespoon hot milk (approx.)

Combine the sugar, butter, vanilla, and enough milk to make a smooth icing of spreading consistency.

GERMAN HAZELNUT RINGS

½ pound sweet butter
1 cup sugar
1 egg yolk (from a medium-size egg)
½ pound unblanched hazelnuts, ground
2 cups sifted all-purpose flour
½ teaspoon salt
Meringue (recipe follows)

Cream the butter with the sugar until light. Blend in the egg yolk, then the hazelnuts.

Sift the flour with the salt. Gradually add to the nut mixture; mix well.

Pat one third of the dough out onto a sheet of waxed paper which has been lightly dusted with flour. Cover with a second sheet of waxed paper; then roll out to ¼-inch thickness. Peel off the top paper, then cut with a 2-inch round cutter. Cut out the centers of the rounds, using a thimble.

Place the rings on a greased cookie sheet, spacing them 1 inch apart. (The centers may be pressed together to form clovers, using 3 or 4 for each cookie.)

Using a pastry tube, or a small spatula and your finger as a guide, place a ribbon of the meringue around the rings, just in the center so that a rim of dough shows on either side. (Put a dollop of meringue in the centers of the clovers.)

Bake in a 325° oven for 12 to 15 minutes, or until lightly browned around the edges.

Makes 5 dozen rings.

Meringue

2 egg whites (from medium-size eggs)
½ cup sugar

Beat the egg whites to stiff peaks; fold in the sugar to make a soft meringue.

SPITZBUBEN

A German specialty traditionally cut with three graduated scalloped cutters, put together with red raspberry or
currant jelly and dusted with powdered sugar. The dough
is the same as for Spritzgeback, but here it is rolled rather
than put through a press. The name Spitzbuben means
"urchins."

>*6 ounces (¾ cup) sweet butter*
>*¾ cup sugar*
>*6 hard-cooked egg yolks (from medium-size eggs)*
>*2 tablespoons kirsch or white rum*
>*1 teaspoon vanilla*
>*2 cups sifted all-purpose flour*
> *Pinch of salt*
> *Red raspberry or currant jelly*
> *Confectioners' sugar*

Cream the butter and sugar until light and fluffy (5
minutes using an electric mixer set at medium speed).
Press the egg yolks through a wire strainer into the
creamed mixture; add the kirsch and vanilla; mix well.

Gradually add the flour and salt, mixing well with a
wooden spoon after each addition. Chill the dough overnight.

Roll out one fifth of the chilled dough at one time
(leaving the remainder refrigerated) between sheets of
waxed paper to ⅛-inch thickness. Carefully peel off the
top paper.

Cut the cookies using scalloped or plain round cutters in three graduated sizes (2½, 1½, and 1 inch). Place
on an ungreased cookie sheet.

Bake in a 350° oven for 8 to 10 minutes, or until the edges are delicately browned. Cool the cookies on racks.

To assemble, spread the bottoms of the middle-size cookies thinly with raspberry jelly and press onto the center of the large cookies; repeat with the small cookies to make three-tiered finished cookies. Dust the tops with sifted confectioners' sugar.

Makes 2½ to 3 dozen three-tiered cookies.

BASLER BRUNSLI

A Swiss chocolate spice cookie, named for the city of Basel. In the traditional form, the rolled cookies are cut into rosettes with small scalloped cutters.

> 2 cups sugar
> ¼ teaspoon salt
> 2 teaspoons cinnamon
> ½ teaspoon cloves
> 1 pound unblanched almonds, ground
> 2 ounces (2 squares) semisweet chocolate, grated
> 2 ounces (2 squares) unsweetened chocolate, grated
> 4 egg whites
> 2 tablespoons kirsch (approx.)
>   Granulated sugar for rolling
>   Glaze (recipe follows)

Combine the sugar, salt, cinnamon, and cloves in a large mixing bowl. Stir in the almonds and chocolates. Add the unbeaten egg whites, one at a time, mixing until blended.

Stir in the kirsch, adding only enough so that the mixture still remains stiff enough for rolling. (It will be somewhat sticky.)

Pat the dough out onto a board sprinkled lightly with sugar. Roll out to slightly less than ½-inch thickness. Cut into rosette shapes or 1½-inch rounds with a cutter.

Place on a well-greased cookie sheet, an inch apart, and let dry overnight at room temperature.

Bake in a 325° oven for 10 to 15 minutes. (They should be firm on the outside but tender within.) Immediately brush the cookies with the Glaze; cool on the cookie sheet.

Makes about 8 dozen.

Glaze

½ cup confectioners' sugar
1 tablespoon boiling water (approx.)

Gradually stir the water into the confectioners' sugar, adding only enough to make a smooth icing.

MONDCHENS

A German sugar cookie shaped into crescent moons with a special cutter.

> ½ *pound sweet butter*
> 1¼ *cups sugar*
> ¼ *teaspoon salt*
>   *Grated rind of 1 lemon*
> 1⅓ *cups sifted all-purpose flour*
> ½ *pound unblanched almonds, ground*
>   1 *egg white slightly beaten with 1 teaspoon water*
>   *Granulated sugar for sprinkling*

Cream the butter. Add the sugar, salt, and lemon rind; cream until light.

Add the flour, then the almonds, mixing with a spoon at first, then finish by kneading lightly with your hands. Chill about 1 hour.

Roll out small portions of the chilled dough at a time on a lightly floured board to ⅛-inch thickness. Cut with a crescent-shaped cookie cutter.

Place on a lightly greased cookie sheet. Brush with the egg white and sprinkle lightly with granulated sugar.

Bake in a 350° oven for 12 to 15 minutes, or until a light tan color.

Makes about 7 dozen medium-size crescents.

CARAWAY KRINGLES

A Scandinavian Christmas cookie, traditionally cut into star shapes. The flavor is unusual; the cookies are delicious.

¼ *pound butter*
1 *cup sugar*
1 *egg*
2 *teaspoons caraway seeds*
2 *cups sifted all-purpose flour*
1½ *teaspoons baking powder*
¼ *teaspoon salt*
3 *tablespoons brandy*
Confectioners' sugar

Beat the butter and sugar together until creamy. Beat in the egg, then the caraway seeds.

Sift the flour with the baking powder and salt; blend in alternately with the brandy. Chill 2 to 3 hours.

Roll out on a lightly floured board to ⅛-inch thickness. Cut with a star-shaped cookie cutter. Transfer the stars to an ungreased baking sheet, spacing them 1 inch apart. Dust the tops generously with confectioners' sugar put through a sieve.

Bake in a 375° oven for 10 to 12 minutes, or until lightly browned.

Makes about 4 dozen 2¾-inch stars.

ZIMTSTERNE
(German Cinnamon Stars)

These traditional German cookies are made of a meringue with a sufficient amount of ground almonds added to turn it into a dough that can be rolled. It is, however, predictably sticky and hard to handle. The cookies are worth the effort.

> *3 egg whites (from medium-size eggs)*
> *Pinch of salt*
> *1 cup fine granulated sugar*
> *1 tablespoon cinnamon*
> *½ teaspoon vanilla*
> *Few drops almond extract*
> *1½ cups unblanched almonds or hazelnuts, ground*
> *Fine granulated sugar and ground nuts*
> *for rolling*

Beat the egg whites with the salt to soft moist peaks. Gradually add the sugar, and continue beating until very thick and the whites hold stiff, shiny peaks.

Take out and set aside 2 tablespoons of the mixture. Sprinkle the cinnamon, vanilla, and almond extract over the top of the remaining egg whites; beat in. Then fold in the ground almonds. (Fold in gently but thoroughly.) Refrigerate, covered, for 30 minutes.

Sprinkle a sheet of waxed paper with fine sugar and ground nuts. Pat out part of the dough onto this mixture. Cover with a second sheet of waxed paper, then roll out to ⅓-inch thickness. Cut with a small star-shaped cutter (1½ inches in diameter).

Arrange the stars 1 inch apart on a well-buttered

cookie sheet. Dot the center of each with a small dollop of the reserved egg white.

Bake in a 275° oven for 25 to 30 minutes, or until a delicate tan color. Cool on the cookie sheet. To remove, drop the sheet on a table or counter (the cookies will spring off).

Makes 3½ to 4 dozen stars.

Note: These cookies are very crisp. They should be ripened in a tightly covered container for 2 to 3 weeks. If soft cookies are preferred, store with a slice of bread.

SPRINGERLE

Here is one of the most famous of German Christmas cookies, embossed and flavored with lemon and anise. The rectangular cookies are formed with a special carved board or rolling pin which produces raised designs on the dough in the shape of Yuletide symbols. Several cookies are formed at one time from a single sheet of dough. These are then cut apart and allowed to dry—so the designs will set—before baking.

4 eggs
1 pound confectioners' sugar
3 to 3½ cups sifted all-purpose flour
1 teaspoon baking powder
1 teaspoon salt
  Grated rind of 1 lemon
  Anise seeds

Beat the eggs until fluffy, using an electric mixer set at medium speed. Gradually beat in the confectioners' sugar; then continue beating on high speed for 20 minutes. (This makes the finished cookies fine-grained and light.)

Sift 3 cups of the flour with the baking powder and salt. Fold into the beaten egg mixture by hand. Add the lemon rind. Knead the dough briefly, add the remaining flour if necessary. (It should be soft and malleable.)

Roll out small portions of the dough on a lightly floured board to about ¼-inch thickness. Dust a Springerle board or rolling pin with flour and press or roll firmly into the dough. Cut the cookies between the designs with a floured knife.

Set 1 inch apart on a lightly greased and floured

cookie sheet, placing a few anise seeds beneath each cookie. Let stand uncovered at room temperature at least 12 hours to dry the tops and set the designs.

Bake in a 275° oven for about 20 minutes, or just until very delicately colored with the appearance of having been iced.

Makes 3 to 6 dozen, depending on size of design.

Note: Store the cookies in a tightly covered container for 2 or 3 weeks to develop flavor.

MORAVIAN CHRISTMAS COOKIES

Baking these molasses-flavored spice cookies is a part of the Christmas tradition for the Moravians who settled in North Carolina.

4 cups sifted all-purpose flour
½ teaspoon salt
1½ teaspoons cinnamon
½ teaspoon ginger
1½ teaspoons cloves
1 cup plus 2 tablespoons brown sugar (packed)
1 cup shortening (butter and lard mixed)
1 cup light molasses
¼ teaspoon baking soda dissolved in
　　½ teaspoon vinegar

Sift the flour, salt, cinnamon, ginger, and cloves into a large mixing bowl. Add sugar and mix well. Work in the shortening with your fingertips, as for pie crust. Add the molasses and baking soda; mix thoroughly. Chill several hours or overnight.

Divide the dough into four portions. Work with one part at a time, keeping the remainder refrigerated. Roll out very, very thin on a lightly floured board. Cut into fancy shapes with cookie cutters.

Bake on a lightly greased cookie sheet in a 350° oven for about 10 minutes, or until the cookies turn an even brown color (not browned around the edges). Immediately slide the cookies from the sheet onto a rack for cooling.

Makes about 6 dozen.

SOFT SPRINGERLE

This is essentially the same recipe as the preceding one, but the addition of the butter keeps these cookies soft. They do not have to be stored for aging.

> ¼ pound butter
> 1 pound confectioners' sugar
> 4 eggs
> 2 teaspoons anise extract or 2 tablespoons anise seed
> Grated rind of ½ lemon
> 4½ cups sifted all-purpose flour
> 2 teaspoons baking powder
> Pinch of salt

Cream the butter. Gradually beat in the sugar. Add the eggs, one at a time, beating well after each addition. Beat in the anise extract (or seed) and lemon rind.

Sift the flour with the baking powder and salt; blend in. Knead the dough briefly, adding more flour if necessary to keep it from sticking to your hands. Chill until firm enough for rolling.

Roll out small portions at a time on a lightly floured board to about ¼-inch thickness.

Flour a Springerle board or rolling pin and press (or roll) firmly into the dough. Cut the cookies between the designs with a floured knife.

Set an inch apart on a lightly greased baking sheet. Let stand at room temperature overnight to dry the tops and set the designs.

Bake in a 325° oven for 10 to 12 minutes, or until a pale yellow. (Watch carefully so that they don't over-brown on the bottoms.)

Makes 3 to 6 dozen, depending on the size of the design.

MOLDED COOKIES

The dough for molded cookies is either shaped into balls, rolled into logs which are refrigerated and sliced, flattened into loaves which are cut after baking, or pressed into a shaped pan. Though the forms are limited, the embellishments range through coatings of nuts or powdered sugar, glazes, and garnishes of candied fruit, sugar sprinkles, or jam.

Included here is Kourabiedes, the Greek shortbread cookie topped with a whole clove to represent the spices brought to the Christ Child by the Magi. Other favorites are Austrian Hussar's Buns, which are similar to our own "thumb-print" cookies; chewy Date-Nut Pinwheels; twice-baked Swedish Almond Toast; and crisp Scotch Shortbread.

PECAN PUFFS

A classic among cookies of this type. In the American South, they are known as Cocoons.

¼ pound butter
2 tablespoons sugar
1 teaspoon vanilla
1 cup sifted cake flour
1 cup pecans, ground
Confectioners' sugar

Cream the butter. Add the sugar and vanilla; beat until light and fluffy. Stir in the flour, then the pecans; mix well. Chill 15 minutes.

Roll the dough into small balls the size of a marble. Place on a greased cookie sheet, spacing them an inch apart.

Bake at 300° for 30 minutes, or until delicately browned.

Roll in confectioners' sugar while warm (not hot), then again when the cookies have cooled.

Makes 2½ dozen.

MEXICAN WEDDING CAKES

These cakes are tinted a pale green to make them festive.

½ pound butter
¼ cup sugar
1 teaspoon vanilla
Green food coloring
2 cups sifted all-purpose flour
1 cup pecans, finely chopped
Confectioners' sugar

Cream the butter. Add the sugar and vanilla; cream until light and fluffy. Add a few drops of food coloring to tint a light green. Add the flour and pecans; mix well.

Roll into 1-inch balls and place an inch apart on an ungreased cookie sheet.

Bake in a 325° oven for 18 to 20 minutes, or until lightly browned.

Remove from the cookie sheet and roll in confectioners' sugar while warm.

Makes about 4½ dozen.

DUTCH SHORTBREAD

This is not a true shortbread, which is made without eggs. Here the dough is rich with hard-cooked egg yolks.

½ pound sweet butter
⅔ cup sugar
¼ teaspoon salt
  Grated rind of 1 lemon
 1 egg
 6 hard-cooked egg yolks
 3 cups sifted all-purpose flour
½ cup sugar mixed with 2 tablespoons cinnamon
⅓ cup finely chopped almonds (blanched or
    unblanched)
 1 egg white, slightly beaten

Cream the butter, sugar, salt, and lemon rind until light and fluffy. Beat in the egg. Press the egg yolks through a wire strainer into the creamed mixture; mix well. Gradually add the flour; blend until smooth.

Form the dough into balls the size of a large marble.

Combine the sugar-and-cinnamon mixture with the almonds. Dip the balls into the egg white, then roll into the sugar mixture.

Bake on a lightly greased cookie sheet at 325° for 18 to 20 minutes, or until golden brown.

Makes 7½ to 8 dozen cookies.

CINNAMON GOLD COOKIES

¼ pound butter
1 cup sugar
4 egg yolks
1 teaspoon vanilla
1½ cups sifted all-purpose flour
2 teaspoons baking powder
½ cup finely chopped pecans
⅛ teaspoon salt
2 teaspoons cinnamon

Cream the butter with the sugar. Add the egg yolks and vanilla; beat well. Sift together the flour and baking powder; stir into the creamed mixture.

Roll the dough into small balls the size of a large marble. Combine the pecans, salt, and cinnamon. Roll the balls of dough in the mixture to coat completely.

Place on a greased cookie sheet about 2 inches apart to allow for spreading. Bake in a 375° oven about 12 minutes, or until the edges start to brown.

Makes 3½ dozen.

PFEFFERNUSSE
(German Peppernuts)

There are dozens of versions for cookies which are called Peppernuts: Pfeffernusse in Germany, Pebernadder in Denmark and Pepparnotter in Sweden. The common theme is the use of pepper along with other spices. This chewy version is made with honey and is glazed after baking.

> 1½ cups honey
> ¼ cup butter
> 1 egg
> 4 cups sifted all-purpose flour
> 1 teaspoon salt
> 1 teaspoon baking powder
> 1 teaspoon baking soda
> 1 teaspoon nutmeg
> 1 teaspoon allspice
> ¾ teaspoon cardamom
> ½ teaspoon black pepper
> ¼ teaspoon finely crushed anise seed
> Honey Glaze (recipe follows)

Heat the honey in a 4-quart saucepan just until thin and hot (do not boil). Stir in the butter; cool to lukewarm.

Beat the egg into the honey mixture.

Sift the flour with the salt, baking powder, baking soda, nutmeg, allspice, cardamom, and pepper. Blend in the crushed anise seed. Stir into the honey mixture. (The dough will be sticky.) Refrigerate 30 minutes to an hour, or until the dough can be easily handled.

Shape the dough into balls about ¾ inch in diameter.

Place on a lightly greased cookie sheet.

Bake in a 350° oven for 13 to 15 minutes, or until only the barest imprint remains when lightly touched. (The cookies should be only faintly browned around the edges.) Cool on a rack.

For glazing, place 12 to 14 cookies in a bowl with 2 tablespoons of the Honey Glaze. Mix with your fingertips to coat all sides (it is not necessary to coat them evenly).

Place the coated cookies on a sheet of waxed paper. Let stand until completely set, and the cookies can be removed easily with the glaze on the bottoms intact. Store in a tightly covered container. The glaze will keep them chewy.

Makes 8 to 9 dozen.

Note: This is an easy way to coat both the tops and bottoms of the cookies at one time. The method gives them an attractive dappled coating.

Honey Glaze

> *2 egg whites*
> *1 tablespoon honey*
> *½ teaspoon finely crushed anise seed*
> *¼ teaspoon cardamom*
> *2 cups sifted confectioners' sugar*

Combine the unbeaten egg whites, honey, and spices in a 1-quart mixing bowl. Gradually beat in the sugar, using a rotary beater, just until well blended.

GINGER NUTS

Soft ginger cookies that are given a festive appearance by rolling them in tiny colored candies or in confectioners' sugar.

> 1 egg
> ½ cup light molasses
> ½ cup shortening, melted
> 3 cups sifted all-purpose flour
> ½ cup sugar
> ½ teaspoon baking soda
> ½ teaspoon salt
> 1 teaspoon cinnamon
> ½ teaspoon cloves
> ½ teaspoon ginger
>   Tiny multicolored candies
>   Confectioners' sugar

Beat the egg well; blend in the molasses and shortening.

Sift the flour with the sugar, baking soda, salt, cinnamon, cloves, and ginger. Gradually add to the molasses mixture, mixing at first with a spoon, then kneading by hand until well blended.

Roll the dough into balls the size of marbles. Roll some in the colored candies to coat completely; leave the remaining balls plain to be rolled in confectioners' sugar after baking.

Place an inch apart on an ungreased baking sheet. Bake in a 350° oven for 10 to 12 minutes. Remove at once from the cookie sheet. Roll the plain cookies in confectioners' sugar while warm.

Makes 6 to 7 dozen.

Note: Store in a tightly covered container with a piece of apple to keep the cookies soft (change frequently).

PEPPARNOTTER
(Swedish Peppernuts)

A Scandinavian version of peppernuts—cookies which include pepper in the list of spices. These are hard and crisp, and require mellowing to take away some of the "bite."

½ pound butter
1 cup sugar
½ cup heavy cream
4 cups sifted all-purpose flour
½ teaspoon baking powder
1 teaspoon baking soda
1 teaspoon cinnamon
½ teaspoon cardamom
1 teaspoon white pepper

Cream the butter and sugar thoroughly. Gradually stir in the cream.

Sift together the flour, baking powder, baking soda, cinnamon, cardamom, and pepper. Add to the butter mixture. Mix together with your fingertips until you have a soft dough that sticks together. Chill the dough 15 minutes.

Form the dough into small balls, about the size of marbles.

Bake on an ungreased cookie sheet at 350° for 18 to 20 minutes, or until firm and lightly browned.

Makes about 10 dozen.

Note: These cookies are peppery when first baked. Store in a tightly covered container at least two weeks to mellow.

GERMAN ANISE COOKIES

The cookies have crinkled, sugary tops and a haunting anise flavor.

> 2 eggs
> 1½ cups dark brown sugar (packed)
> ¼ teaspoon salt
> ½ teaspoon baking soda dissolved in 1 tablespoon hot water
> 2 cups plus 2 tablespoons sifted all-purpose flour
> 1 tablespoon whole anise seeds
> Granulated sugar

Beat the eggs until very light, using an electric mixer set at a medium speed. Gradually add the sugar (any soft lumps will blend in); then continue beating for 15 minutes. (The mixture should be very thick.)

Stir in the salt and dissolved baking soda. Add the flour and anise seeds; fold in until well blended.

With lightly greased hands, form the soft mixture into small balls the size of hickory nuts (slightly less than ¾ inch in diameter). As the balls are made, place them in a pie plate which contains a layer of sugar; then turn the balls to coat evenly.

Arrange the coated balls 1½ inches apart on a greased cookie sheet to allow for spreading.

Bake at 375° for 8 to 10 minutes. (They will puff up during baking, then flatten and crackle when done. They will be soft when taken from the oven, but quickly firm up.)

Makes 9 dozen.

Note: These cookies become crisp when stored; their flavor improves with aging.

BLACK WALNUT COOKIES

A cousin to the previous recipe, this cookie is flavored with black walnuts, not licorice-tasting anise.

3 eggs
1½ teaspoons water
1 pound brown sugar
3 cups sifted all-purpose flour
¼ teaspoon salt
½ teaspoon baking soda
½ cup black walnuts, chopped

Beat the eggs with the water until thick and lemon-colored, using an electric mixer set at medium speed. Gradually add the sugar (any soft lumps will blend in) and continue to beat until very thick, about 15 minutes longer.

Sift the flour with the salt and baking soda. Mix in the walnuts. Fold into the egg mixture one quarter at a time; blend just until well combined.

Form into balls the size of hickory nuts (about ¾ inch) with lightly greased hands. (If the dough is too sticky, work in a little more flour.)

Place at least an inch apart on an ungreased cookie sheet. Bake in a 350° oven for 10 to 12 minutes. (They will puff up during baking, then crackle on top when done.)

Makes about 12 dozen.

Note: These cookies improve when aged. Store them in a tightly covered container. Add a slice of bread a week before using to soften them.

FILBERT BUTTER BALLS

Nuggets of dough rolled in chopped filberts and made colorful by garnishing with red or green candied cherries.

¼ pound sweet butter
¼ cup sugar
1 egg yolk (from a medium-size egg)
1 tablespoon white rum or lemon juice
½ teaspoon vanilla
1 cup sifted all-purpose flour
1 egg white
½ cup finely chopped filberts (hazelnuts)
*   Red and green candied cherries, cut in quarters*

Cream the butter with the sugar until fluffy. Add the egg yolk, rum, and vanilla; blend well. Stir in the flour. Cover the bowl and refrigerate 3 to 4 hours, or overnight.

Roll into small balls, using about ¼ rounded teaspoonful for each. Beat the egg white slightly in a saucer. Roll the balls through the egg white, coating just the middle; then roll through the filberts in the same manner. Place 1 inch apart (uncoated-side down) on a lightly greased cookie sheet, and press a quarter of a cherry into the top.

Bake in a 325° oven for 10 to 12 minutes.
Makes about 3½ dozen.

FRENCH ALMOND COOKIES

Shaped like almonds, then garnished with almond halves, when baked, these cookies are crackly and crisp.

> ½ *pound butter*
> 1¼ *cups granulated sugar*
> 1¼ *cups brown sugar (packed)*
> 2 *eggs*
> 1 *tablespoon honey*
> 1 *teaspoon almond extract*
> ½ *pound unblanched almonds, ground*
> 3 *cups sifted all-purpose flour*
> 1 *teaspoon baking soda*
> ⅔ *cup blanched almond halves (approx.)*

Cream the butter with the sugars. Beat in the eggs one at a time. Stir in the honey and almond extract. Blend in the ground almonds.

Sift the flour with the baking soda. Add to the almond mixture gradually; mix, then knead with your hands until the flour is well blended. Chill briefly if necessary for easier handling.

Pinch off pieces of the dough, about the size of a large marble (¾ inch). Roll between the palms of your hands into an oval shape. Place on a lightly greased cookie sheet. Space the cookies 1½ to 2 inches apart. Press a blanched almond half into the center of each cookie.

Bake in a 350° oven 13 to 15 minutes, or until golden brown and the almonds are lightly toasted.

Makes about 12 dozen.

Note: This recipe makes a large quantity; however, they will keep well for months.

HUSARENKRAPFERL
(Austrian Hussar's Buns)

An Austrian specialty similar to our own "thumb-print" cookies. However, the end of a wooden spoon is used and the depression filled with apricot jam. In addition the cookies are coated with chopped blanched almonds and dusted attractively with confectioners' sugar.

¼ pound sweet butter
¼ cup sugar
1 egg yolk
1 cup sifted all-purpose flour
1 egg white, slightly beaten
⅓ cup finely chopped almonds
Confectioners' sugar
Apricot jam or preserves

Cream the butter with the sugar until light. Add the egg yolk; mix well. Blend in the flour. Chill the dough 30 minutes.

Pinch off pieces of the dough and form into 1-inch balls. (You should have 18.)

Beat the egg white until foamy. Dip the balls of dough into the egg white, then roll in the chopped almonds. As the balls are coated, set them aside on a plate. Make a depression in the center of each with the end of a wooden cooking spoon. Refrigerate until firm.

Place 1 inch apart on an ungreased cookie sheet. Bake in a 350° oven for about 15 minutes, or until lightly golden. Remove to racks to cool.

Dust the tops lightly with confectioners' sugar and fill the depressions with apricot jam.

Makes 18.

Note: If cookies are to be stored, fill with the jam just before serving.

BRYSSELKAX
(Swedish Brussels Cakes)

A refrigerator cookie that is actually Swedish, although named for the capital of Belgium. When baked, these crisp cookies have an attractive edge rimmed with almonds.

> ¼ *pound sweet butter*
> ½ *cup sugar*
> 1 *egg yolk*
> ½ *teaspoon vanilla*
> 1½ *cups sifted cake flour*
> 1 *teaspoon baking powder*
> ½ *teaspoon salt*
> 1 *egg white*
> ⅓ *cup finely chopped blanched almonds*
> 2 *tablespoons sugar for coating*

Cream the butter. Gradually add the sugar, creaming well. Add the egg yolk and vanilla; beat well.

Sift together the flour, baking powder, and salt. Add to the creamed mixture and knead with your hands to make a smooth dough.

Divide the dough into two parts. Place on waxed paper and shape into long rolls 1¼ inches in diameter, about 8 inches long. Wrap in the waxed paper and chill at least 1 hour, or until the dough is firm enough to slice.

Just before baking, beat the egg white slightly and brush the chilled cookie rolls. Combine the almonds and remaining 2 tablespoons sugar. Roll the coated dough in the mixture, pressing the nuts in firmly.

Slice about ¼ inch thick and place on a lightly greased cookie sheet, spacing the cookies about 1 inch apart.

Bake in a 350° oven for about 8 minutes, or until faintly browned around the edges.

Makes about 6 dozen.

DATE-NUT PINWHEELS

An old-time icebox cookie that is favored during the holidays, though it is made the year around.

> 1 pound chopped dates
> 1 cup granulated sugar
> 1 cup water
> 1 cup chopped pecans
> 1 cup shortening
> 2 cups brown sugar (packed)
> 3 eggs
> 4 cups unsifted all-purpose flour
> 1 teaspoon salt
> ½ teaspoon baking soda

Combine the dates, granulated sugar, and water in a heavy saucepan. Cook over low heat for 10 minutes, stirring frequently, or until thickened. Remove from heat and cool; then stir in the pecans.

Cream the shortening with the brown sugar until light and fluffy. Add the eggs one at a time, beating well after each addition.

Sift the flour with the salt and baking soda. Add to the egg mixture; mix well. Chill the dough thoroughly.

Divide the dough in half. Roll out one part at a time on a well-floured board into a rectangle to a thickness slightly less than ¼ inch. Spread evenly to the edges with half the date-nut mixture. Roll up from the long side as for a jelly roll. Wrap in waxed paper and chill overnight.

When ready to bake, cut the rolls into slices slightly less than ¼ inch thick, using a thin, sharp knife. Place about 2 inches apart on a greased cookie sheet.

Bake in a 400° oven for 10 to 12 minutes, or until lightly browned.

Makes about 6 dozen pinwheels.

BELGRADER BROT

In spite of the name (which derives from Belgrade, the capital of Yugoslavia), these are German Christmas specialties. The spicy fruit- and nut-laden dough is baked in long loaves, then glazed and sliced when removed from the oven.

> 3 medium-size eggs
> 1 cup sugar
> 2 cups sifted all-purpose flour
> 1 teaspoon baking powder
> ½ teaspoon baking soda
> ¼ teaspoon salt
> 2 teaspoons cinnamon
> ¼ teaspoon cloves
> ¼ teaspoon cardamom
> Grated rind of ½ lemon
> ¼ pound mixed candied citron and orange peel, cut fine
> 1⅓ cups unblanched almonds, ground
> Glaze (recipe follows)
> Colored sugars

Beat the eggs until fluffy (use an electric mixer set at medium speed). Gradually add the sugar; continue beating until very thick and almost white.

Sift the flour with the baking powder, baking soda, salt, cinnamon, cloves, and cardamom. Gradually add to the egg mixture (with mixer set at low); mix thoroughly. Fold in the lemon rind, candied fruit, and almonds.

Divide the dough into three parts. Form into long narrow rolls, 2 inches wide and ¾ inch thick. Place on a greased and floured cookie sheet. Pat the tops lightly to even. (They should be spaced 2 to 3 inches apart to allow for spreading.)

Bake in a 300° oven for 20 to 25 minutes, or until lightly browned.

Remove the cookie sheet from the oven. Spread the Glaze over the tops of the rolls and sprinkle with colored sugars as desired. Cool about 5 minutes, then cut each roll into 1-inch slices. Set on a rack to cool.

When cooled, store the cookies in a tightly covered container. They keep well.

Makes 8 dozen slices.

Glaze

1¼ cups confectioners' sugar
2 tablespoons boiling water (approx.)

Stir the sugar and water until smooth, using just enough to make the consistency of heavy cream.

SWEDISH ALMOND TOAST

These cookies are baked twice: first in long loaves, then in slices which are returned to the oven until they are dry and crisp.

½ pound sweet butter
1 cup sugar
2 medium-size eggs
3 tablespoons sour cream
3 cups sifted all-purpose flour
1 teaspoon baking powder
¼ teaspoon baking soda
¼ teaspoon salt
½ cup finely chopped blanched almonds
    Pearl sugar or crushed loaf sugar

Cream the butter with the sugar until light and fluffy. Beat in the eggs one at a time, reserving about 1 tablespoon of egg white for glazing. Blend in the sour cream.

Sift the flour with the baking powder, baking soda, and salt. Add gradually to the egg mixture, beating only until smooth. Fold in the almonds; knead lightly until smooth.

Divide the dough into four parts. Form into long narrow rolls, about 1½ inches in diameter. Place about 2 inches apart on a lightly greased cookie sheet. Press with your hands to flatten slightly. Beat the reserved egg white slightly with a fork; brush over the tops of the flattened dough. Sprinkle lightly with the pearl sugar.

Bake in a 350° oven for 20 minutes, or until ivory-colored and fairly firm. Remove from the oven and cut into ½-inch slices. Lay the slices, cut-side down, on clean, ungreased cookie sheets. Return to a 250° oven and bake for 20 to 30 minutes, or long enough to toast lightly and dry out.

Makes about 8 dozen.

Note: These will keep well stored in a tightly covered container.

KOURABIEDES
(Greek Almond Cookies)

A Greek specialty, each cookie is formed into an almond shape and studded with a whole clove, a reminder of the spices brought by the Magi to the Christ Child.

½ pound butter
¼ cup confectioners' sugar
1 egg yolk
2 tablespoons brandy
½ teaspoon vanilla
½ cup finely chopped blanched almonds
2 cups sifted all-purpose flour
½ teaspoon baking powder
36 whole cloves
Confectioners' sugar for dusting

Cream the butter. Gradually add the sugar and beat until fluffy. Add the egg yolk, brandy, and vanilla; beat again until very light. Stir in the almonds.

Sift the flour with the baking powder. Blend into the creamed mixture, mixing by hand to form a soft, smooth dough. Chill the dough 30 minutes, or until it can be handled easily.

Shape level tablespoonfuls of the dough into small oval cakes (like an almond). Place 1 inch apart on an ungreased baking sheet. Insert a whole clove in the center of each.

Bake in a 325° oven for 25 to 30 minutes, or until sandy colored, not brown. Cool on a rack.

For serving, arrange the cookies on a platter in layers, dusting each layer generously with sifted confectioners' sugar.

Makes about 3½ dozen.

SCOTCH SHORTBREAD

A rich, buttery cookie with a long history, it remains the pride of Scottish baking. The dough contains rice flour which adds to the sandiness of the texture. It is pressed into a pan for baking, then cut into wedges for serving.

1½ cups sifted all-purpose flour
½ cup unsifted rice flour*
½ cup fine granulated sugar
½ pound sweet butter (cold)
Granulated sugar for sprinkling

* Rice flour can be purchased in Oriental grocery stores. An equal amount of all-purpose flour may be substituted.

Combine both of the flours and sugar in a bowl. Slice the cold butter into the flour mixture. Mix with your fingertips to coarse crumbs. Then work the dough until smooth and well blended by kneading with your hands.

Divide the dough in half. Press into two 8-inch round cake pans. Use a small spatula to smooth the tops. Prick the entire surface with a fork (as you would for a pastry shell).

Bake in a 300° oven for 45 minutes, or until faintly colored. Remove from the oven and sprinkle the tops lightly with granulated sugar. Cool on racks for 10 minutes, then cut each shortbread into 16 wedges. (Do not remove from the pans.) Cool completely, then cover tightly for storing.

Makes 32 thin wedges.

TASSIES

Like miniature pecan pies. Margarine may be used for the pastry, but butter makes the crust more flavorful.

> ¼ *pound sweet butter or margarine*
> 1 *package (3 ounces) cream cheese*
> 1 *cup sifted all-purpose flour*
> 2 *medium-size eggs*
> 1½ *cups dark brown sugar (packed)*
> 2 *tablespoons butter, melted*
> ¼ *teaspoon vanilla*
> *Pinch of salt*
> ½ *cup chopped pecans*

Soften the butter and cream cheese at room temperature and blend together. Add the flour and blend well.

Divide the mixture into 24 balls, about 1 inch in diameter. Press into tiny muffin cups, 1¾ inches in diameter (measured across the top), covering the bottom and sides evenly.

Combine the eggs and sugar, stirring with a fork to blend (do not beat). Stir in the melted butter, vanilla, and salt.

Put ½ teaspoon of the chopped pecans in each of the pastry-lined cups. Fill (no more than three-quarters full) with the egg mixture, and sprinkle the remaining pecans on top.

Bake in a 350° oven for about 30 minutes. (The cookies will be done when the crust is golden brown.)

Makes 24.

HAND-SHAPED COOKIES

Considered the treasures of any cookie assortment, hand-shaped cookies take patience and skill to produce. They are formed into various shapes: logs, crescents, rings, S's, or pretzels. In most instances, however, the dough is quickly and easily made.

This selection includes the wreath-shaped Berliner Kranser from Norway, garnished with glittering sugar crystals; Zitronen Ringe, a lemon-flavored German cookie shaped into rings; and Vanillekringler, a Danish specialty twisted into a pretzel shape and iced with a vanilla glaze. The prize of the collection is Hungarian Kipfel, a delicate rolled pastry which encloses a delicious ground hazelnut filling.

MANDEL KRABELI
(Swiss Almond Crescents)

A Swiss specialty which is made with grated chocolate and candied orange peel as well as almonds.

> 2 egg whites (*from medium-size eggs*)
> ⅛ teaspoon salt
> ½ cup sugar
> 2 ounces (½ bar) German's sweet chocolate, grated
> ½ ounce (½ square) unsweetened chocolate, grated
> ½ pound blanched almonds, finely chopped
> 1 ounce (about 3 tablespoons) candied orange peel, finely chopped
> Glaze (recipe follows)

Beat the egg whites with the salt until stiff. Gradually add the sugar and continue beating until very stiff and glossy. Fold in the chocolate, almonds, and orange peel; mix thoroughly.

Using a level tablespoon, form 24 mounds, placing them on a sheet of waxed paper. Shape the mounds into ovals by rolling them between sugared and floured hands, turning the ends to form into crescents. (If the mounds are too sticky to handle, let stand several minutes until slightly dry.)

Place the crescents on a well-greased cookie sheet, spacing them 1½ inches apart.

Bake in a 325° oven for 18 to 20 minutes, or until dry on the outside but moist and soft in the center. (They will harden somewhat as they cool; don't overbake.)

Immediately brush the cookies with the Glaze, then

quickly but carefully remove to a rack for cooling. (They are fragile. If the cookies stick, return the cookie sheet to the oven to reheat briefly.)

Makes 24 crescents.

Glaze

½ *cup confectioners' sugar*
⅛ *teaspoon vanilla*
1 *tablespoon boiling water* (*approx.*)

Combine the sugar and vanilla. Gradually add enough boiling water to make a smooth icing that spreads without running. (Use a pastry brush for spreading on the cookies.)

ALMOND CRESCENTS

The addition of kirsch lightens the dough and makes the cookies tender.

> ½ *pound sweet butter*
> 3 *tablespoons fine granulated sugar*
> 1 *tablespoon vanilla sugar**
> 1 *tablespoon kirsch or white rum*
> 2 *cups unsifted all-purpose flour*
>   *Pinch of salt*
> ¾ *cup blanched almonds, ground*
>   *Fine granulated sugar for rolling*
>   *Vanilla sugar for dusting*

* Vanilla sugar: Bury a vanilla bean in a quart jar of fine granulated sugar. Let stand a few days before using.

Cream the butter. Add both of the sugars and beat until light and fluffy. Blend in the kirsch. Stir in half of the flour and the salt. Then add the almonds and the remaining flour. Chill overnight.

Break off small pieces of the dough; on a board lightly dusted with sugar, roll out with your hands into strips the thickness of a pencil. Cut into 3-inch lengths and turn the ends to shape into crescents.

Arrange the crescents an inch apart on a lightly buttered cookie sheet. Bake in a 350° oven for about 15 minutes, or until delicately browned. (They should remain almost white.)

Carefully transfer the cookies to a tray. While still slightly warm, dust the tops with vanilla sugar (put through a wire strainer).

Makes about 5 dozen crescents.

HOERNCHEN

A short German cookie.

> ½ *pound butter*
> ¾ *cup sugar*
> 1 *egg*
> 1 *teaspoon vanilla*
> 2¼ *cups unsifted all-purpose flour*
> ½ *pound unblanched almonds, ground*
>   *Red- and green-colored sugars or tiny*
>   *multicolored candies*

Cream the butter and the sugar. Add the egg and vanilla; blend well. Stir in the flour and ground almonds.

Pinch off a piece of the dough the size of a walnut; roll between the palms of your hands into strips the thickness of your little finger. Form into a crescent shape by turning the ends.

Dip one side of the crescent into colored sugars or candies. Place the uncoated side down on an ungreased cookie sheet.

Bake in a 350° oven for about 15 minutes, or until lightly browned.

Makes about 6 dozen crescents.

Note: For variation, the dough may be formed into S shapes. Use a little more dough and roll slightly longer. (To form the German S, shape the dough into a reverse-S shape.)

HUNGARIAN KIPFELS

These delicate pastries are filled with ground hazel-nuts. They may be included in a Christmas cookie assortment or served as a finger dessert for an open house buffet.

> 1 cup sifted all-purpose flour
>   Pinch of salt
> ¼ pound sweet butter (cold)
> 2 egg yolks (from medium-size eggs), beaten
>   slightly
> 2 tablespoons white rum
> 2 egg whites
>   Pinch of salt (for filling)
> ½ cup sugar
> ½ teaspoon vanilla
> 1 cup (about 3½ ounces) ground hazelnuts
>   (measured after grinding)
>   Confectioners' sugar

Combine the flour and salt in a mixing bowl. Cut the butter from the stick in small pieces, dropping them into the flour mixture. Work with your fingertips or a pastry blender until the consistency of cornmeal. Add the beaten egg yolks and rum; mix lightly but well to form a smooth dough (it should feel like pie dough).

Form the dough into 36 small balls. Place on a plate, cover, and refrigerate 3 to 4 hours, or overnight.

When ready to bake the kipfels, beat the egg whites with the salt until foamy. Gradually add the sugar and continue beating until the mixture is very thick. Add the vanilla. Fold in the ground nuts; set aside. (This is the filling.)

Remove 6 balls at a time from the refrigerator. Roll

into thin rounds (about 2½ inches in diameter) between sheets of waxed paper. Put a teaspoon of the filling in the centers of the pastries. Fold one side over, then the other to enclose the filling. Press the ends lightly to seal.

Place the filled pastries on an ungreased cookie sheet, spacing them an inch apart. Bake in a 350° oven for 15 minutes, or until lightly browned. Remove from the cookie sheets while warm. When cool, dust with confectioners' sugar.

Makes 36 kipfels.

BERLINER KRANSER

Although the name suggests that these cookies are German, the recipe is from Norway. The hand-rolled dough is formed into pencil-like strips, then made into wreaths by looping the ends. They are decorated in the traditional manner with coarse sugar which glitters like ice crystals.

> *2 hard-cooked egg yolks*
> *2 raw egg yolks*
> *½ cup sugar*
> *½ teaspoon almond extract*
> *½ pound butter*
> *2½ cups sifted all-purpose flour*
> *1 egg white, slightly beaten*
> *Pearl sugar**

* If pearl sugar is not available, decorate the knot with bits of candied cherries and citron to resemble holly. (Although not traditional, these cookies are more attractive.)

Press the hard-cooked egg yolks through a wire strainer into a small bowl. Add the raw egg yolks, sugar, and almond extract; blend.

Using a pastry blender, cut the butter into the flour until fine. Add the egg yolk mixture; knead to form a smooth dough. If necessary, chill the dough until it can be handled easily.

Break off small pieces of the dough (about a rounded teaspoonful). Roll out with your hands on an unfloured surface into strips the thickness of a pencil, about 6 inches long. Form into a ring, bringing one end over and through to form a single knot. (The ends should overlap about ½ inch.)

Dip the wreaths as they are made into the egg white, then into the pearl sugar. Place an inch apart on an ungreased cookie sheet.

Bake in a 350° oven for about 10 minutes, or until delicately browned at the edges. Cool slightly before removing from the sheet, as they are delicate.

Makes about 6 dozen wreaths.

FINSKA PINNAR
(Finnish Fingers)

Finger-shaped cookies with a garnish of chopped almonds and sparkling sugar.

> 2½ cups sifted all-purpose flour
> ½ cup sugar
> ½ pound butter, slightly softened
> 1 teaspoon almond extract
> 1 egg, slightly beaten
> ½ cup finely chopped blanched almonds
> Pearl sugar or crushed loaf sugar

Combine the flour and sugar. Cut in the butter with a pastry blender until the mixture forms crumbs the size of a pea. Sprinkle the almond extract over the top. Knead the mixture lightly but well to distribute the flavoring.

Divide the dough into eight parts. With lightly floured hands, roll the dough into long strips about the thickness of your little finger. Cut into 2-inch lengths; press the tops with your finger to flatten slightly.

Place on an ungreased cookie sheet, spacing them about 1 inch apart. Brush the tops with the beaten egg; sprinkle with the almonds and pearl sugar.

Bake in a 350° oven for 12 to 15 minutes, or until a delicate golden brown.

Makes about 6 dozen.

ZITRONEN RINGE
(German Lemon Rings)

A German specialty, but not as well known as numerous other German cookies.

> 6 ounces (¾ cup) sweet butter
> 1 cup sugar
> 3 medium-size eggs
> 2 cups sifted all-purpose flour
> Grated rind of ½ lemon
> 1 tablespoon white rum or lemon juice
> 1 egg white, slightly beaten
> Pearl sugar or crushed loaf sugar

Cream the butter and sugar until light. Add the eggs one at a time and beat until fluffy. Add the flour, lemon rind, and rum; mix well. Chill the dough thoroughly.

Break off a small portion of the dough. Roll out with hands on a lightly floured board into a strip the thickness of a pencil; cut into 5-inch lengths and shape into rings, pressing the ends together. Brush with the egg white and sprinkle with pearl sugar.

Arrange the rings 1 inch apart on a lightly greased cookie sheet. Bake in a 350° oven for 10 to 12 minutes, or until only delicately browned. Remove from the cookie sheet while still warm.

Makes 4 to 4½ dozen rings.

Note: For variety, part of the dough can be formed into pretzel shapes.

KONJAKSKRANSAR
(Swedish Cognac Rings)

Konjakskransar are a pleasant challenge to the cookie baker. A double strand of dough is twisted together like twine, then formed into a ring.

> *3 cups sifted cake flour*
> *¾ cup sugar*
> *½ teaspoon salt*
> *½ pound sweet butter*
> *3 tablespoons cognac (approx.)*

Sift the flour, sugar, and salt into a bowl. Cut in the butter until the mixture resembles coarse meal. Sprinkle the cognac over the mixture, a tablespoon at a time, mixing with a fork until the mixture holds together, adding additional cognac if necessary. Press the dough together to form a ball. Chill the dough until it can be handled easily.

Pinch off a piece of the dough, using about a rounded teaspoonful. Roll out with your hands on an unfloured surface into pencil-like strips about 8 inches long. Pull the ends together, side by side, then twist the two together like twine. Shape into a ring, pinching the ends securely. Place on a ungreased baking sheet, about an inch apart.

Bake in a 375° oven for 5 to 7 minutes, or until set. They should remain white.

Makes about 6 dozen.

SWISS BUTTER S's

½ *pound butter*
½ *cup sugar*
  4 *egg yolks (from medium-size eggs)*
    Grated rind of 1½ lemons
  2 *cups less 2 tablespoons sifted all-purpose flour*
    Flour and sugar for rolling
  1 *egg yolk mixed with 1 tablespoon cream*
    Sugar for sprinkling

Cream the butter and the sugar. Add the egg yolks one at a time, beating after each addition. Add the lemon rind. Add the flour; mix well.

Divide the dough into thirds; then divide each third into 6 parts (to facilitate handling). Roll out one portion at a time on a board lightly dusted with a mixture of flour and sugar. Use your hands and roll the dough into a strip slightly less than the thickness of your little finger. Cut into 3-inch lengths.

Transfer the strips to an ungreased cookie sheet and shape into S's. Space an inch apart. Brush with the egg yolk and cream mixture; sprinkle with sugar. Refrigerate on the cookie sheet 20 minutes.

Bake in 425° oven for 5 minutes, or until the edges are lightly browned. Cool a few minutes to set, then remove from the cookie sheet.

Makes about 7 dozen.

VANILLEKRINGLER
(Danish Vanilla Pretzels)

A Danish specialty with a vanilla glaze.

> ½ pound butter
> 4 cups sifted all-purpose flour
> 4 egg yolks
> 1 tablespoon heavy cream
> 1 cup plus 2 tablespoons sugar
> 2 teaspoons vanilla
> Vanilla Glaze (recipe follows)

Cut the butter into the flour using a pastry blender.

Beat the egg yolks with the cream, sugar, and vanilla until very thick. Stir into the flour mixture, then knead with your hands to form a smooth dough which does not stick to your fingers.

Break off small pieces of dough (about a rounded teaspoonful). Roll out on a lightly floured board into pencil-like strips about 7 inches long. Pull the ends as if to make a ring, but overlap to form a pretzel shape. Press the ends lightly.

Arrange an inch apart on an ungreased cookie sheet. Let stand overnight uncovered at room temperature.

Bake in a 350° oven for 10 to 12 minutes, or until delicately browned at the edges.

Ice while warm with Vanilla Glaze.

Makes about 4 dozen.

Vanilla Glaze

1 cup sifted confectioners' sugar
1 teaspoon vanilla
1 tablespoon heavy cream (approx.)

Combine the sugar, vanilla, and enough cream to make a smooth icing of spreading consistency.

COOKIE-PRESS COOKIES

Known as spritz, these decorative butter cookies are shaped by forcing a soft dough through a cookie press. The name comes from the German word which means to squirt. In the Old World method the dough is pressed through a small fancy tip. With a modern cookie press, which includes a series of additional flat, design plates, a greater variety of designs is possible.

The Spritzgeback, from Germany, uses the original method to form wreaths, S's, and candles. Sweden's Spritsar and the Royal Crowns of Norway (which are decorated with "jewels" of red and green candied cherries) are representative of those that are shaped with decorative plates.

SPRITZGEBACK
(German Spritz Cookies)

The Old World method of making spritz cookies is required for this German version. The dough is forced through a small rosette or star tip into a continuous ribbon, then cut and hand-shaped into dainty wreaths, backward S's (the German way), and candles. They are then beautifully finished by decorating with candied fruits or by dipping into melted chocolate, then nuts or chocolate sprinkles.

6 ounces (¾ cup) sweet butter
¾ cup sugar
6 hard-cooked egg yolks (from medium-size eggs)
2 tablespoons kirsch or white rum
1 teaspoon vanilla
2 cups sifted all-purpose flour
  Pinch of salt
  Red candied cherries and citron
  Melted semisweet chocolate
  Chopped pistachios
  Chocolate sprinkles

Cream the butter and sugar until light and fluffy (5 minutes using an electric mixer set at medium speed). Press the egg yolks through a wire strainer into the creamed mixture; add the kirsch and vanilla; mix well.

Gradually add the flour and salt, mixing well with a wooden spoon after each addition. Chill the dough 15 minutes.

Holly Wreaths: Force the dough through a cookie

press, using a decorator tip (rosette), onto an unfloured board in one long, continuous spiral strip. (The press should be held at a 45° angle. Start at the edge of the board and work toward the center, leaving a generous space between the concentric rings of dough.) Cut into 4½-inch lengths. Join the ends and form into wreaths. Decorate the joint with a tiny bit of candied cherry and place a sliver of citron on each side.

Transfer the formed cookies carefully to a lightly greased cookie sheet, leaving a 1-inch space between them. Bake at 350° for 10 to 12 minutes, or until the edges begin to turn a delicate brown. Cool the cookies on the sheet. (They are too fragile to remove while hot.)

German S's and Candles: Force the dough through the cookie press in the same manner as directed for the Holly Wreaths, but use a star-shaped decorator tip. For German S's, cut the strip into 3½-inch lengths and form into a reverse S-shape (the German way). For Candles, leave the ribbons of dough in straight lengths, cutting them 2½ inches long. Bake and cool as given for the Holly Wreaths.

When cool, dip the ends of the S's into slightly cooled melted chocolate (a bit of butter will give it gloss), then into chopped pistachios. Dip only one end of the Candles into the chocolate, then into chocolate sprinkles.

Makes about 6 dozen wreaths, German S's, and candles.

SPRITSAR
(Swedish Spritz Cookies)

Swedish Spritsar were originally shaped (as in the previous German recipe) into rings or S's by putting the soft dough through a simple star tube. With the modern cookie press, additional shapes (such as Christmas trees, rosettes, and serrated bars) may be formed for variety.

> 1 pound butter
> 1 cup sugar
> 1 egg
> 2 egg yolks
> 1 teaspoon vanilla
> 2 teaspoons grated orange rind
> 4½ cups sifted all-purpose flour
> Red and green food coloring (optional)
> Colored sugars, tiny multicolored candies, silver dragees and candied fruit

Cream the butter. Add the sugar gradually and cream until light and fluffy. Beat in the egg and egg yolks, vanilla and orange rind. Gradually blend in the flour to make a soft dough. (Tint part of the dough pink or green with food coloring if desired.)

Force the dough through a cookie press onto an ungreased cookie sheet, forming into desired shapes. Decorate with the colored sugars, candies, dragees, or candied fruit.

Bake in a 350° oven for 10 to 12 minutes, or until set, the edges just barely turning color.

Makes 14 to 16 dozen.

Note: For Christmas trees, tint part of the dough lightly with green food coloring. Use the tree design plate; sprinkle with the multicolored candies for "lights" and place a silver dragee on top for a "star."

BUTTER STICKS

Easily made, the dough for these cookies is put through a press (using a serrated design plate) into long continuous strips, then cut after baking.

> ¾ cup butter
> ¾ cup confectioners' sugar, sifted
> 1 egg yolk
> 1 tablespoon lemon juice
> 2 cups sifted all-purpose flour
> ¼ teaspoon salt
> ¼ teaspoon baking powder
> ½ cup (about 1½ ounces) ground almonds (measured after grinding)
> 1 teaspoon grated lemon peel

Cream the butter, confectioners' sugar, and egg yolk in an electric mixer set at medium speed. Stir in the lemon juice.

Sift the flour with the salt and baking powder. Mix in the almonds and lemon peel. Add to the creamed mixture, stirring by hand until well blended. Chill the dough for several hours to blend the flavors.

Allow the dough to warm to a consistency so that it is soft enough to put through a cookie press.

Using a serrated design plate, force the dough through the press onto an ungreased cookie sheet into long continuous strips.

Bake in a 375° oven for 5 to 8 minutes, or until the strips are set and the bottoms are lightly browned. Remove from the oven and cut into 2-inch lengths before removing from the sheet to cooling racks.

Makes 4 to 5 dozen sticks.

LEMON CRISPS

½ *pound butter*
½ *cup sugar*
½ *cup light brown sugar (packed)*
2 *tablespoons lemon juice*
1 *egg*
1 *teaspoon grated lemon rind*
2½ *cups sifted all-purpose flour*
¼ *teaspoon salt*
¼ *teaspoon baking soda*
   Candied lemon peel and citron

Cream the butter. Gradually add both the sugars and lemon juice; cream well.

Beat in the egg and lemon rind.

Sift together the flour, salt, and baking soda. Gradually blend into the creamed mixture to make a soft dough.

Force the dough through a cookie press onto an ungreased cookie sheet, forming into desired shapes. Decorate the tops with bits of candied peel and citron.

Bake in a 400° oven for 7 to 10 minutes, or until the edges are faintly browned.

Makes about 7 dozen.

ROYAL CROWNS

A Norwegian cookie (perhaps this country's most well known) pressed into a crown shape and decorated with "jewels" of red and green candied cherries.

> ¼ pound butter
> ¼ cup sugar
> ⅛ teaspoon salt
> ½ teaspoon orange extract
> 2 hard-cooked egg yolks
> 1 cup sifted all-purpose flour
> Red and green candied cherries

Cream the butter. Gradually add the sugar, salt, and orange extract; beat until fluffy. Force the egg yolks through a wire strainer into the creamed mixture. Gradually blend in the flour.

Using the crown flat design plate of a cookie press, force the dough through the press onto an ungreased cookie sheet. Decorate the points with bits of the candied cherries.

Bake in a 375° oven for 7 to 10 minutes, or until set but not brown.

Makes about 3 dozen.

TIVOLIS

Danish spritz cookies with a peanut butter accent.

½ *pound butter*
2 *tablespoons peanut butter*
1 *cup confectioners' sugar, sifted*
1 *egg*
1 *teaspoon vanilla*
½ *teaspoon almond extract*
2¼ *cups sifted all-purpose flour*
½ *teaspoon baking powder*

Cream the butter with the peanut butter. Gradually add the sugar; blend well. Beat in the egg, vanilla, and almond extract.

Sift the flour with the baking powder. Gradually blend into the creamed mixture.

Force the dough through a cookie press onto an ungreased cookie sheet forming into desired shapes.

Bake in a 375° oven for 10 to 12 minutes, or until delicately browned.

Makes about 6 dozen.

BAR COOKIES

These cookies are easily prepared by spreading the dough in a pan or on a cookie sheet, then cutting into bars or squares after it is baked.

Among the perennial favorites are the chewy Date-Nut Squares and the Chinese Chews which are rolled in confectioners' sugar. Also there is the delicious crisp Janhagel from Holland, which has a scattering of sliced almonds on top; and English Rum Cakes, a fruitcake cookie with a rum-flavored frosting.

JANHAGEL

An exceptionally crisp Dutch cookie topped with sliced, unblanched almonds.

> 1⅓ cups sifted all-purpose flour
> ½ cup sugar
> ½ teaspoon cinnamon
> ¼ pound sweet butter (cold)
> 1 egg yolk
> 1 egg white, slightly beaten
> ¼ cup sugar mixed with ½ cup sliced
>   unblanched almonds

Combine the flour, sugar, and cinnamon in a mixing bowl. Cut the butter from the stick into small pieces, dropping them into the flour mixture. Work the mixture with your fingertips until small crumbs are formed. Add the egg yolk and work it in until the yolk is well distributed, then knead into a ball.

Press the dough into a 10 x 12-inch metal baking pan, using your hands. (The thickness of the dough should be as uniform as possible, especially along the edges.) Brush the top with the egg white; then sprinkle with the sugar-and-almond mixture.

Bake in a 350° oven for 15 to 20 minutes, or until lightly browned.

Remove from the oven. Let cool a few minutes, then cut into 2 x 1-inch rectangles. (A chef's knife or a cleaver will cut neater slices; press the blade down through the dough firmly.) Finish cooling on a rack before removing the cookies from the pan.

Makes 4½ dozen.

SWEDISH FRUIT SQUARES

These easily made cookies are baked in a sheet, then cut into squares.

> ¼ *pound butter*
> 1 *cup sugar*
> 1 *egg*
> ¼ *cup orange juice*
> 2½ *cups sifted all-purpose flour*
> ½ *teaspoon salt*
> 1 *teaspoon baking soda*
> ½ *teaspoon cinnamon*
> ½ *teaspoon nutmeg*
> 1 *cup mixed candied fruit*
> 1 *cup raisins*
> ½ *cup pecans, coarsely chopped*

Cream the butter with the sugar and egg. Stir in the orange juice. (The mixture will look curdled.)

Sift the flour, salt, baking soda, cinnamon, and nutmeg; stir into the creamed mixture. Add the candied fruit, raisins, and pecans; mix well.

Spread the mixture into a greased 15 x 10 x 1-inch jelly-roll pan; flatten with floured hands to even.

Bake in a 400° oven for 10 to 12 minutes, or until golden brown. (Test with a wooden pick.)

Cut while slightly warm into 1½-inch squares, but do not remove from the pan until cool.

Makes about 6 dozen.

TOFFEE BARS

With a chocolate and pecan topping.

½ pound butter
1 cup brown sugar (packed)
1 egg
1 teaspoon vanilla
2 cups sifted all-purpose flour
½ pound sweet chocolate, melted
1 cup pecans, chopped

Cream the butter. Gradually add the sugar; beat until light and fluffy. Add the egg and vanilla; blend until smooth. Gradually add the flour; mix well.

Spread the dough in an ungreased 15 x 10 x 1-inch jelly-roll pan. Press evenly with a pancake turner.

Bake in a 350° oven for 25 minutes, or until brown around the edges. Remove from the oven and immediately spread the melted chocolate over the top. Scatter the pecans evenly over the chocolate. Tip the pan slightly from side to side to insure that the nuts will stick in the chocolate.

When the chocolate is set, cut into 2 x 1-inch bars. When completely cool, cover the pan with foil for storing.
Makes 6 dozen bars.

ALMOND BARS

½ cup sugar
1 cup chopped blanched almonds
½ cup shortening
1 egg
1 egg yolk
1 cup sifted all-purpose flour
1 tablespoon lemon juice
1 teaspoon grated lemon peel
1 egg white, slightly beaten

Combine the sugar and almonds. Remove and set aside ½ cup.

Cream the shortening with the remaining sugar-almond mixture. Beat in the egg, then the egg yolk; beat well.

Add the flour, lemon juice, and peel; mix thoroughly.

Spread the mixture in a greased 8-inch square baking pan. Brush the top with the egg white. Sprinkle with the reserved sugar-almond mixture.

Bake in a 325° oven for 30 minutes. Cool slightly, then cut into 2 x 1-inch bars. Cool completely before removing from the pan.

Makes 32 bars.

CHINESE CHEWS

An old-time favorite filled with dates and nuts.

>¾ cup sifted all-purpose flour
>1 cup sugar
>1 teaspoon baking powder
>¼ teaspoon salt
>1 cup dates, cut in small pieces
>1 cup pecans, coarsely chopped
>2 eggs, well beaten
>Confectioners' sugar

Sift the flour, sugar, baking powder, and salt into a bowl. Add the dates and pecans; mix well to coat evenly. Add the beaten eggs; mix thoroughly.

Spread in a greased 15 x 10 x 1-inch baking pan. Bake in a 375° oven for 20 minutes, or until fairly firm.

Cut into 2 x 1-inch bars (or slightly smaller) while warm and roll in confectioners' sugar.

Makes at least 6 dozen bars.

DATE-NUT SQUARES

2 cups dates
1 cup walnuts
½ cup sifted all-purpose flour
¾ cup sugar
1 teaspoon baking powder
¼ teaspoon salt
2 eggs
4 tablespoons margarine, melted and cooled
    Confectioners' sugar

Combine the dates and walnuts; put through a food grinder.

Sift the flour with the sugar, baking powder, and salt. Add the ground dates and nuts; mix well to coat.

Beat the eggs until light. Stir in the margarine. Add the date mixture and mix thoroughly.

Turn the mixture into a well-greased and floured 9 x 9 x 2-inch baking pan. Bake in a 350° oven for about 40 minutes. The top should be a medium-brown color. (Use a pick inserted in the center for testing.)

Cool in the pan set on a rack, then cut into 1½-inch squares and roll in confectioners' sugar.

Makes 3 dozen squares.

ENGLISH RUM CAKES

Like miniature frosted fruitcakes.

> *4 medium-size eggs*
> *1 teaspoon vanilla*
> *1 cup confectioners' sugar*
> *1 cup sifted all-purpose flour*
> *½ teaspoon salt*
> *1 teaspoon baking powder*
> *½ pound candied pineapple, finely chopped*
> *½ pound candied cherries, finely chopped*
> *1 pound dates, finely chopped*
> *Rum Frosting (recipe follows)*

Beat the eggs well; add the vanilla.

Sift the sugar with the flour, salt, and baking powder. Add the chopped pineapple, cherries, and dates; mix well to coat. Stir into the beaten eggs; mix well. Turn into a greased and floured 9 x 9-inch baking pan.

Bake in a 325° oven for about 1 hour. (Use a pick inserted in the center for testing.) Cool in the pan set on a rack.

Frost the top with Rum Frosting. Cover the pan tightly with foil and store in a cool place for at least a week to age. Cut into 1-inch squares when ready to serve.

Rum Frosting

⅓ cup butter (soft)
1½ cups sifted confectioners' sugar
1 tablespoon rum (approx.)

Mix the butter and sugar to a crumb consistency, using your fingertips. Stir in enough rum to make a spreading consistency.

Makes 81 cakes.

SWEDISH FRUIT BALLS

Baked in a pan, then scooped out and rolled into balls.

2 tablespoons butter
2 eggs
1 teaspoon vanilla
1 cup brown sugar (packed)
6 tablespoons unsifted all-purpose flour
⅛ teaspoon baking soda
1 cup chopped mixed candied fruits
Confectioners' sugar

Melt the butter in a metal 9-inch square baking pan. Tilt the pan to coat the bottom evenly; set aside.

Beat the eggs slightly. Stir in the vanilla. Combine the brown sugar, flour, and baking soda; mix in the candied fruits. Stir into the eggs; mix well. Pour into the buttered pan; do not stir.

Bake in a 350° oven for 20 minutes.

Remove to a rack and let stand until cool enough to handle, but still warm. Remove the mixture by tablespoonfuls and roll into small balls; then roll in confectioners' sugar to coat.

Makes about 25 balls.

DROP COOKIES

The soft dough for these cookies is dropped from a spoon into mounds which either hold their shapes or spread into thin wafers.

American Lizzies and Christmas Rocks, which are laden with fruits and nuts, are among the favorites of this group. There are also Anisplatzchen, those famous German anise drops, which form a thin white cap while drying and baking; and Havreflarn, the crisp, toffee-like Swedish oatmeal cookie that was created at a time when almonds were scarce.

LIZZIES

An American fruitcake cookie which may be eaten immediately after baking, or stored for aging.

½ *pound raisins*
½ *cup bourbon whiskey*
¼ *pound butter*
½ *cup brown sugar (packed)*
2 *eggs, lightly beaten*
1½ *cups sifted all-purpose flour*
1½ *teaspoons baking soda*
1½ *teaspoons cinnamon*
½ *teaspoon cloves*
½ *teaspoon nutmeg*
½ *pound red candied cherries, cut in quarters*
½ *pound candied pineapple, coarsely cut*
½ *pound pecans, broken*
Red and green candied cherries for garnish

Soak the raisins in the whiskey for at least 1 hour.

Cream the butter and the brown sugar until light. Gradually blend in the eggs.

Sift the flour with the baking soda, cinnamon, cloves, and nutmeg. Add the candied cherries and pineapple, mixing well to separate and coat; then add the pecans. Stir into the butter mixture. Add the raisins and whiskey; mix well.

Drop by teaspoonfuls onto a greased cookie sheet at least 1½ inches apart. Garnish at least half of the cookies with a small piece of red or green candied cherry each. (It will make the cookies look more festive than if they are left plain.)

Bake in a 325° oven for about 10 minutes, or until golden and slightly firm to the touch. Remove the cookies immediately from the baking sheets and cool on racks. Store in tightly covered containers with sheets of waxed paper between the layers.

Makes 8½ to 9 dozen.

Note: These soft, chewy cookies may be eaten immediately, but improve with age and keep well for months.

CHRISTMAS ROCKS

Similar to Lizzies, but walnuts and dates are used here.

¼ pound butter
½ cup sugar
3 eggs
*1 teaspoon baking soda dissolved in 1 table-
spoon warm water*
2 cups sifted all-purpose flour
1 teaspoon cinnamon
½ teaspoon cloves
1 pound walnuts, broken
1 pound pitted dates, coarsely cut
Red and green candied cherries

Cream the butter and sugar until light. Beat in the eggs one at a time. Stir in the dissolved baking soda.

Sift the flour with the cinnamon and cloves. Add the walnuts and dates, mixing well to coat. Add to the egg mixture; mix well.

Drop from a teaspoon into mounds on a greased cookie sheet at least 1 inch apart. Garnish the tops with a small piece of red or green candied cherry.

Bake in a 375° oven for 8 to 10 minutes, or until golden. Remove the cookies immediately from the baking sheet and cool on racks. Store in a tightly covered container with sheets of waxed paper between the layers.

Makes 8½ to 9 dozen.

Note: These cookies improve in flavor when stored at least 2 weeks.

FINNISH CARDAMOM COOKIES

½ cup dark corn syrup
¼ pound butter
 1 teaspoon cardamom
¼ teaspoon cloves
¼ teaspoon ginger
 2 teapsoons grated orange rind
 1 egg
 2 cups sifted all-purpose flour
½ cup sugar
½ teaspoon baking soda
    Light corn syrup
    Tiny multicolored candies

Combine the dark corn syrup, butter, cardamom, cloves, ginger and orange rind in a saucepan. Bring to a boil over medium heat, stirring until the butter is melted. Remove from the heat and cool slightly.

Beat the egg in a large mixing bowl until light. Gradually stir in the syrup mixture; blend well.

Sift the flour with the sugar and baking soda; add all at once to the syrup mixture; blend well.

Drop by teaspoonfuls onto a well-greased cookie sheet. Bake in a 350° oven for 8 to 10 minutes, or until slightly browned. Brush immediately with the light corn syrup, and sprinkle with colored candies. Remove to a rack for cooling.

Makes about 4½ dozen.

WHISKEY SHORTCAKES

These are very rich cakes—the type that melt in your mouth.

> ½ *pound butter*
> 1 *egg yolk*
> ½ *cup confectioners' sugar*
> ¼ *cup whiskey*
> 1 *tablespoon grated orange rind*
> 1½ *cups sifted all-purpose flour*
> *Orange marmalade*
> *Confectioners' sugar for dusting*

Cream the butter until fluffy (use an electric mixer set at medium speed). Add the egg yolk, confectioners' sugar, and whiskey. Continue beating for 5 minutes.

Sprinkle the orange rind over the batter. Gradually add the flour, stirring with a wooden spoon until smooth.

Drop from a teaspoon onto an ungreased cookie sheet. (They may be placed close together; they spread very little.) Drop a tiny bit of marmalade onto the top of each cookie.

Bake in a 350° oven for 10 to 15 minutes, or until delicately browned. Transfer to a tray and let stand until cool.

Dust the tops with confectioners' sugar (put through a sieve).

Makes 4 dozen.

CREAM CHEESE DROPS

With a chocolate morsel atop each one.

½ *pound sweet butter or unsalted margarine*
1 *package (3 ounces) cream cheese*
1 *cup sugar*
1 *teaspoon vanilla*
2 *cups sifted all-purpose flour*
½ *cup finely chopped pecans*
⅓ *cup semisweet chocolate morsels (approx.)*

Allow the butter and cream cheese to soften at room temperature.

Cream together the softened butter, cream cheese, and sugar. Add the vanilla; mix well. Gradually add the flour, beating in thoroughly. Mix in the pecans.

Drop from a teaspoon onto a lightly greased cookie sheet. Decorate the tops with chocolate morsels, one for each cookie.

Bake in a 375° oven for about 10 minutes. (The cookies should be very lightly browned.)

Makes 8 dozen small cookies.

ANISPLATZCHEN
(German Anise Drops)

A thin Bavarian cookie which forms its own crisp cap of frosting. A classic among traditional German Christmas cookies.

    3 eggs
    1 cup plus 2 tablespoons sugar
    1¾ cups sifted all-purpose flour
    ½ teaspoon baking powder
    ½ teaspoon salt
    1 teaspoon anise extract

Beat the eggs until fluffy (use an electric mixer at medium speed). Gradually beat in the sugar; then continue beating 20 minutes longer.

Sift the flour with the baking powder and salt. Add to the egg mixture and continue beating for 3 minutes (at low speed). Blend in the anise extract.

Drop by teaspoonfuls onto a lightly greased and floured cookie sheet, spacing them about 2 inches apart. Swirl the batter with the back of the teaspoon to form cookies about 1½ inches in diameter. Let stand at room temperature overnight to set. (Do not cover.)

Bake in a 325° oven for about 10 minutes, or until a creamy golden color on the bottom. (Over-baking will make these cookies hard; the bottoms should be somewhat soft and cakelike.)

Cool on racks and store in an airtight container. (They will keep well for several weeks.)

Makes about 7½ dozen 1½-inch cookies.

BISCOTTI AL PIGNOLI
(Italian Pine Nut Cookies)

Italian drop cookies garnished with pine nuts.

4 eggs
1½ cups sugar
    Grated rind of ½ lemon
2 cups sifted all-purpose flour
¼ teaspoon salt
    Confectioners' sugar
¼ cup pine nuts (approx.)

Combine the eggs and sugar in the top of a double boiler; beat until frothy, using an electric mixer set at medium speed. Place over simmering water and beat until the mixture is warm. Remove from the heat and continue beating until the eggs are foaming and the bubbles are fine-textured.

Add the lemon rind. Sift together the flour and salt; gradually fold in.

Drop by half teaspoonfuls on a greased and floured cookie sheet, leaving an inch between them. Swirl with the back of the spoon into circles. Dust the cookies with confectioners' sugar put through a sieve. Sprinkle a few pine nuts (3 or 4) on top. Let stand 10 minutes.

Bake in a 325° oven for 10 minutes, or until a creamy golden color on the bottom. (Over-baking will make these cookies hard.)

Makes about 11 to 12 dozen.

LINCOLN CRISPS

A crunchy drop cookie made with coconut, walnuts, and cornflakes.

> 1 cup sugar
> 2 tablespoons butter
> ½ teaspoon salt
> 1 teaspoon vanilla
> ⅔ cup shredded dry coconut
> ⅔ cup broken walnuts
> 4 cups cornflakes (unfrosted)
> 2 egg whites, stiffly beaten

Cream the sugar and butter. Stir in the salt, vanilla, coconut, walnuts, and cornflakes; mix lightly.

Fold in the stiffly beaten egg whites, mixing until the mixture looks moistened. (It will be crumbly.)

Using a teaspoon, press the mixture into the spoon by pressing it against the side of the bowl. Then drop the mixture onto a greased cookie sheet, using your finger as an aid to form small mounds.

Bake in a 300° oven for 15 minutes, or until the coconut turns a golden brown. Cool slightly before removing from the cookie sheet.

Makes about 3 dozen.

BUTTER PECAN ROUNDS

¼ *pound butter*
⅔ *cup brown sugar (packed)*
1 *egg yolk*
1 *cup sifted all-purpose flour*
⅛ *teaspoon cream of tartar*
    Pinch of salt
½ *cup chopped pecans*
½ *cup pecan halves (approx.)*

Cream the butter. Gradually add the sugar; blend until creamy. Stir in the egg yolk.

Sift the flour with the cream of tartar and salt. Add the chopped pecans. Stir into the creamed mixture.

Drop by teaspoonfuls on an ungreased cookie sheet; top each with a pecan half.

Bake in a 325° oven for 12 to 15 minutes, or until lightly browned around the edges.

Makes about 3 dozen.

HAVREFLARN
(Swedish Oatmeal Lace Cookies)

Lace cookies are made from a thin dropped batter which spreads and separates as it bakes into lacelike wafers. The Swedes make two versions: one with chopped almonds; the other with oatmeal instead of nuts, a matter of economy when almonds were scarce. The results were so pleasing that the improvised version persists. For the lacy effect, pinhead oatmeal works best, but rolled oats make delicious cookies, too.

> 6 ounces (¾ cup) butter
> 2 cups brown sugar (packed)
> ½ teaspoon salt
> 2 cups uncooked oatmeal or old-fashioned
>   rolled oats
> 1 egg
> 1 teaspoon vanilla

Melt the butter in a saucepan. Remove from the heat and stir in the brown sugar, salt, and oatmeal. Beat the egg slightly with the vanilla; blend in.

Drop the mixture by level measuring teaspoonfuls onto a well-greased cookie sheet. (They should be spaced 2 inches apart.)

Bake in a 350° oven for 5 to 7 minutes, or until golden brown. Allow the cookies to remain on the cookie sheet until they set and can be removed easily. Cool on racks.

Makes about 6 dozen.

CHOCOLATE LACE COOKIES

These lace wafers contain both oatmeal and almonds. The undersides are glazed with chocolate after they have been baked.

    ¼ pound butter
     1 cup sugar
    ¼ cup dark corn syrup
     1 teaspoon vanilla
    ¾ cup sifted all-purpose flour
    ½ teaspoon salt
    ½ teaspoon baking powder
    ¼ cup milk
     1 cup uncooked old-fashioned rolled oats
     1 cup chopped blanched almonds
     6 ounces (6 squares) semisweet chocolate

Cream the butter with the sugar until light. Stir in the corn syrup and vanilla.

Sift the flour with the salt and baking powder. Add to the creamed mixture alternately with the milk, beating until smooth. Stir in the rolled oats and almonds.

Drop by rounded measuring teaspoonfuls onto a cookie sheet lined with ungreased aluminum foil. (Space 3 inches apart to allow for spreading.)

Bake in a 325° oven for 10 minutes, or until the edges are well browned and the cookies are bubbling.

Let cool completely, then peel away the foil.

Melt the chocolate over hot (not boiling) water. Brush or spread the melted chocolate thinly over the undersides of the wafers. Let stand until set in a cool place.

Store the cookies in a tightly covered container (in a cool place) with waxed paper between the layers.

Makes 6 dozen 2½-inch wafers.

MERINGUES AND MACAROONS

Meringues (or kisses) and macaroons are a special type of drop cookie that is made with egg whites. Meringues are light and crisp and often contain chopped fruits and nuts; macaroons are chewy with ground nuts.

Included here are Hazelnut Macaroons, which are garnished with a puff of meringue and a whole hazelnut; Forgotten Meringues, which contain chocolate morsels; Amaretti, the classic Italian macaroon; and Wittenkusse, Austria's Widow's Kisses, made with walnuts, candied cherries, and citrus peel.

FORGOTTEN MERINGUES

Easy to bake, these meringues made with chocolate morsels are left in the oven overnight to dry.

> *2 egg whites*
> *Pinch of salt*
> *⅔ cup sugar*
> *1 teaspoon vanilla*
> *1 cup (6 ounces) semisweet chocolate morsels*

Beat the egg whites until foamy. Add the salt and continue beating until the whites stand in soft peaks. Gradually add the sugar, beating thoroughly until the mixture forms very stiff peaks.

Sprinkle the vanilla and chocolate morsels over the top; fold in.

Drop by small teaspoonfuls onto a lightly buttered cookie sheet. (They may be placed close together, as they will not spread.)

Place in a 350° oven and immediately turn the oven off. Let the cookies dry in the oven overnight.

Makes about 5 dozen.

DATE-NUT FINGERS

Crisp meringue coating, chewy inside.

3 egg whites
¼ teaspoon salt
1¾ cups confectioners' sugar
1 tablespoon flour
2 cups broken pecans
1 cup chopped dates
1 teaspoon vanilla

Beat the egg whites with the salt until stiff. Sift the confectioners' sugar with the flour; beat in a tablespoon at a time. Continue beating until the meringue stands in very stiff peaks. Fold in the pecans, dates, and vanilla.

Drop by the tablespoonful onto a greased cookie sheet, using your finger as a guide to form into 3-inch lengths.

Bake in a 300° oven about 18 minutes, or until they feel crisp to the touch. (They should be only faintly colored.) Cool on the cookie sheet.

Makes about 4 dozen meringues.

COCONUT KISSES

2 egg whites
½ cup sugar
½ teaspoon white vinegar
¾ cup shredded dry coconut (see Note)

Beat the egg whites until foamy. Gradually add the sugar, teaspoon by teaspoon, beating until the mixture forms stiff peaks. Add the vinegar and fold in the dry coconut.

Drop by teaspoonfuls 2 inches apart onto a well-greased cookie sheet. Bake in a 275° oven for 20 minutes. (The cookies should feel dry to the touch and hold their shape.) Cool on the cookie sheets.

Makes about 3½ dozen.

Note: The coconut must be dry; if moist, dry out in an oven set at a low temperature, then cool before using.

BEACON HILL COOKIES

A chocolate meringue-type cookie.

  1 cup (6 ounces) semisweet chocolate morsels
  2 egg whites
  ½ cup sugar
  ½ teaspoon vinegar
  ½ teaspoon vanilla
  ¾ cup chopped walnuts

Melt the chocolate morsels, stirring, in a double boiler set over hot water; set aside to cool until barely warm.

Beat the egg whites until foamy. Add the sugar, a teaspoon at a time, and continue beating until the mixture forms stiff peaks. Add the vinegar and vanilla toward the end.

Fold in the melted chocolate and walnuts; blend lightly but evenly.

Drop by small teaspoonfuls onto a greased cookie sheet. (Space the mixture 2 inches apart to allow for spreading.)

Bake in a 350° oven for 10 minutes. (They will be crisp on the outside, moist within.) Cool the cookies on the baking sheet.

Makes about 5 dozen.

ALMOND MACAROONS

These macaroons have a distinct almond flavor due to the fact that half of the almonds are left in their natural state—with skins intact—while the rest are blanched.

4 egg whites
½ teaspoon white vinegar
1 cup sugar
¼ pound unblanched almonds, ground
¼ pound blanched almonds, ground

Beat the egg whites until foamy, using an electric mixer at medium speed. Add the vinegar and continue beating until they are stiff. Gradually add the sugar, a tablespoon at a time; then continue beating 7 to 8 minutes longer (on high speed), or until very stiff and the sugar is completely dissolved. Fold in the ground almonds.

Drop by teaspoonfuls onto a greased cookie sheet, spacing them 1 inch apart.

Bake at 275° for 25 minutes, or until firm. (They should be only faintly colored.) Cool on the cookie sheet. To remove, drop the sheet on a table or counter (the cookies will spring off).

Makes about 5 dozen macaroons.

HAZELNUT MACAROONS

Chewy, with a puff of meringue and a whole hazelnut in the center.

> *4 egg whites*
> *1 teaspoon lemon juice*
> *1½ cups sifted confectioners' sugar*
> *¼ pound unblanched hazelnuts, ground*
> *¼ pound blanched almonds, ground*
> *¼ pound whole hazelnuts (approx.) for garnishing*

Beat the egg whites until foamy, using an electric mixer at medium speed. Add the lemon juice and continue beating until stiff. Gradually add the sugar, beating continuously. When all of the sugar has been added, continue beating 7 to 8 minutes longer (on high speed), or until very stiff.

Remove ½ cup of the meringue for icing; then fold the nuts into the remainder.

Drop by teaspoonfuls onto a well-greased cookie sheet, spacing them 2 inches apart. Make a small depression with a teaspoon on the top of each meringue. Then drop a bit of icing into the depression and press a hazelnut into the center.

Bake in a 275° oven for about 25 minutes, or until firm. (They should be only faintly colored.) Cool the macaroons on the sheet. To remove, drop the sheet on a table or counter (the cookies will spring off).

Makes about 4 dozen.

AMARETTI
(Italian Macaroons)

2 egg whites
½ teaspoon almond extract
½ pound blanched almonds, ground
1 cup sugar
Dash of salt
Confectioners' sugar

Beat the egg whites until stiff but not dry, adding the almond extract toward the end. Combine the almonds, sugar, and salt; fold in.

Drop by teaspoons onto a lightly buttered and floured cookie sheet. Sprinkle with confectioners' sugar (put through a sieve). Let stand uncovered at room temperature for 2 hours. (This will dry the tops and help the macaroons keep their shape during baking.)

Bake in a 300° oven about 25 minutes, or until golden brown.

Makes 32 macaroons.

CHRISTMAS BON BONS

Nuggets of ground dates and nuts given a Christmas wrap of pink- or green-tinted meringue.

> 1 cup pitted dates
> ½ cup walnuts
> ½ teaspoon vanilla
> 2 egg whites
>   Dash of salt
> ⅔ cup sugar
>   Red and green food coloring

Put the dates and walnuts through a food grinder. Add the vanilla; blend well. Shape into 36 small balls.

Beat the egg whites with the salt until stiff. Gradually add the sugar and continue beating until very stiff and glossy.

Divide the mixture in two parts; tint half with a few drops of green food coloring to obtain a delicate shade. Repeat the process with red food coloring.

One by one dip the date-nut balls into the tinted meringue, using a teaspoon. Place on a greased cookie sheet, swirling the tops of the meringue attractively.

Bake in a 250° oven for 30 minutes, or until the tops are delicately browned.

Makes 36.

WITENKUSSE
(Austrian Widow's Kisses)

A sliver of glazed cherry atop each kiss merely hints at the chewy fruits enclosed within the crisp outer shell.

> 4 egg whites
> 2¼ cups confectioners' sugar
> ½ cup walnuts, ground
> 1 ounce candied cherries, chopped fine
> 1 ounce candied orange peel, chopped fine
> 1 ounce candied lemon peel, chopped fine
> Candied cherries for garnishing

Beat the egg whites until stiff. Stir in the confectioner's sugar, then continue beating until very stiff and shiny.

Fold in the walnuts, candied cherries, orange and lemon peel.

Drop by half-teaspoonfuls onto a greased baking sheet. (They may be spaced close together; they do not spread.) Decorate each top with a small piece of candied cherry.

Bake in a 275° oven for 20 minutes, or until set. Remove from the sheet while hot.

Makes 9½ dozen 1½-inch kisses.

Note: There should be a generous ½ cup of candied fruits, measured before chopping.

CHRISTMAS CANDIES

COOKING AND STORING

Although a wide variety of candies may be bought for the Christmas holidays, as in cookie baking, there is tremendous joy and satisfaction in producing one's own product from pure, natural ingredients.

Some of the recipes given here are simple, require little or no cooking, and are considered "foolproof." For others, which require cooking, the controlled amount of crystallization of the sugar (as in creamy candies) or the absence of sugar crystals (in solid mixtures such as chewy and hard candies) is the major concern. The recipes and the guidelines which follow are designed to deal with these concerns.

Helpful Tips

1. The most important consideration in cooking candies is temperature control. Errors of overcooking are reduced by the use of a candy thermometer which measures both temperature and consistency. The thermometer is much more accurate than the old-fashioned method of dropping small portions of the syrup in cold water to test for consistency. Combining both tests provides the precision of the modern method with the fun of the old-fashioned way.

Before using a thermometer, it is wise to test its accuracy. Place it in a saucepan of water; bring the water to the boiling point and let it bubble a few minutes. The thermometer should read 212° when viewed at eye level. Adjust the temperatures in the recipes if the reading is not perfect.

Note: If there is excess moisture in the air, the mixture should be cooked to a firmer state—1 to 2 degrees higher than those prescribed.

2. The following guidelines are useful for hand-testing in cold water. Only the first one—a sugar syrup—is tested by dropping the syrup from a spoon or fork over the boiling mixture. The rest require that about a half-teaspoon of syrup be dropped into a cup of cold tap water and gathered together with the fingers. Use a clean spoon and fresh water for each testing, and remove the syrup from the heat to prevent overcooking.

COLD WATER TEST

Thread (230–234°): syrup spins a 2-inch thread when a little is dropped from a spoon or fork (not in water).

Soft Ball (234–240°): syrup forms a soft ball in water, which flattens when it is picked up.

Firm Ball (244–248°): syrup forms a firm ball in water, which holds its shape unless pressed.

Hard Ball (250–265°): syrup forms a hard ball in water, which holds its shape but is pliable.

Soft Crack (270–290°): syrup separates into hard strands which are brittle in water but soft and pliable when removed, and make a clinking sound when tapped on the side of the container holding the water.

Hard Crack (300–310°): syrup forms brittle strands, which remain brittle when removed from the water and are not sticky.

3. The candy mixture should be cooked in a heavy pan, which will prevent scorching, and in a pan with a large enough capacity to prevent the contents from boiling over. The recipes specify minimum pan sizes, although slightly larger ones can be used. In general, a quart capacity is needed for every cup of sugar. Those candies

made with a large quantity of cream or milk, or those that contain soda, are exceptions. For these the foaming of the mixture is excessive and a larger pan is required.

4. The ingredients should be blended together before they are put on the heat, then stirred carefully until the sugar is completely dissolved. This will prevent sugar crystals from collecting on the sides of the pan, one of the major faults in poorly prepared candies.

In some recipes a buttered pan is recommended; in others, covering the pan will dissolve unwanted crystals at the initial stage of cooking.

If at any time crystals appear, wipe them down with a pastry brush dipped in warm water.

5. Candies made with milk or cream should be cooked at medium or low heat; they sometimes require stirring to prevent scorching. Stirring should be done slowly to prevent crystallization.

Candies made with water (i.e., without milk or cream) can often be cooked slightly more rapidly once the sugar has dissolved, but then must be watched carefully and cooked slowly for the last 20° to prevent discoloring.

6. Divinity, seafoam, and nougat are made by beating a hot syrup mixture into beaten egg whites. The important concern here is humidity. Unless the day is clear and the humidity low, the mixture may not become firm enough to hold shape.

Note: An electric mixer is a necessary tool because the syrup must be poured into the egg whites while the mixture is beaten continuously.

Humidity is also important when making pulled mints or taffy. With excessive humidity, mints will not turn creamy; taffy may not stiffen. In addition, these candies must be allowed to cool undisturbed until they can be handled for pulling, or the mixture will turn into a hard, sugary mass. (If this does happen, the mixture may be returned to a clean saucepan and recooked with additional water.)

7. For all firm, chewy, and hard candies, the last of the syrup should be left in the pan to avoid crystallizing.

8. Fudge, penuche, and similar creamy candies are usually allowed to stand until they are lukewarm (110°), then they are beaten. If you do not use a thermometer, let the mixture stand until your hand can be placed comfortably on the bottom of the pan.

This cooling before beating insures a creamy-smooth product. Stirring or jarring the syrup during this cooling period may also cause it to crystallize.

For beating, either a wooden spoon or an electric mixer may be used. However, the spoon is preferred, since in the final stages the syrup quickly turns from syrup to fudge, and the signs are easier to detect. A simple stirring, lifting and folding of the mass is all that is necessary. When the mixture is ready to be turned out, it will thicken and begin to lose its gloss. If it is not beaten long enough, the mixture will not set; if it is beaten too much it may become sugary and hard. Should this happen, it can be remedied by turning the mixture out onto a board and kneading it until it is smooth and creamy.

At its proper consistency, the beaten mixture will look like creamy butter frosting, and the swirls on the top will hold their shape.

Storing

Most homemade candies keep well for several weeks when stored in airtight containers. Keep the types separate so that they retain their basic characteristics: soft, chewy, or hard.

Fudge, penuche, and similar creamy candies are best stored in the pans in which they are cooled. When the candy is completely cooled, the pan should be wrapped tightly in aluminum foil. Stored in a cool, dry place at room temperature, these candies can be kept for at least a month.

Dropped cream candies should be stored in tightly covered containers, and although they keep well in a cool place, they tend to dry faster on the exterior than do those stored as described above. Of all such candies, divinity and seafoam are the most delicate and should be eaten shortly after they are made.

Chewy candies, such as taffy, caramels, and nougat, are individually wrapped after cooling to keep them from spreading and sticking to each other. It is particularly important that these candies remain free of moisture, which makes them sticky. A tightly covered container is an absolute must, as is the cool, dry storage place. (Never store in the refrigerator.)

Toffees, brittles, and other hard candies should also be stored in a cool, dry place. They keep for months. If they have been properly cooked and completely cooled before storing, they will not stick together.

Uncooked candies made with melted chocolate keep exceedingly well. A cool temperature is important; they should be stored in layers separated with waxed paper to prevent softening and sticking.

Except for the candies made with gelatin, all candies may be frozen for months if they are properly stored in tightly sealed containers. When removing them from the freezer, let the container stand several hours at room temperature before opening it. This will prevent moisture from collecting on the candies.

CREAMY CANDIES

This category includes several kinds of fudge, penuche, pralines, divinity, and mints.

Among the fudge recipes are chocolate Million Dollar Fudge, made so easily that it competes with old-time versions; White Satin Christmas Fudge, colorfully filled with red and green candied cherries; and rich Opera Cream Fudge. And there is Seafoam, similar to Divinity but made with brown sugar; Pulled Butter Mints, which are pulled like taffy but magically become creamy; and a smooth chocolate confection of French origin, known as Truffles.

MILLION DOLLAR FUDGE

This is one of the most treasured of fudge recipes: it is easy to make (no beating), dark and creamy, and comes out perfectly every time.

> 1 package (12 ounces) semisweet
>   chocolate morsels
> 3 bars (12 ounces) German's sweet chocolate,
>   broken up
> 1 jar (7 to 8 ounces) marshmallow creme
> 4½ cups sugar
>   Pinch of salt
> 2 tablespoons butter
> 1 can (14½ ounces) evaporated milk
> 2 cups almonds, coarsely chopped

Combine the chocolate morsels, sweet chocolate, and marshmallow creme in a large bowl. Set aside.

Combine the sugar, salt, butter, and evaporated milk in a heavy 4-quart saucepan. Stir over medium heat until the mixture comes to a full boil; then continue boiling and stirring for 6 minutes.

Pour the boiling syrup over the chocolate-marshmallow mixture. Stir until the chocolate is melted and the mixture is smooth. Then stir in the almonds.

Pour into a lightly buttered 12 x 8 x 2-inch pan. Let stand until firm, then cut into 1-inch squares. Store in a tightly sealed container.

Makes about 5½ pounds.

OLD-FASHIONED COCOA FUDGE

Creamy and only lightly flavored with cocoa.

3 cups sugar
4 tablespoons cocoa
Pinch of salt
1½ cups milk
1 tablespoon butter
1 teaspoon vanilla

Combine the sugar, cocoa, and salt in a heavy 4-quart saucepan. Stir in the milk.

Place over low heat, and cook, stirring constantly, until the sugar is dissolved. Then continue cooking without stirring to 234°, or until a small amount dropped into cold water forms a soft ball.

Remove from the heat; add the butter and, without stirring, cool to lukewarm (110°).

Add the vanilla and beat until the fudge is thick and loses its shine.

Quickly pour into a lightly buttered 8-inch square pan. When firm, cut into squares.

Makes about 1½ pounds.

Note: This fudge is soft and may require refrigeration. Cover tightly.

COCOA PEANUT BUTTER FUDGE

A delicious fudge with an accent of peanut butter flavor. The cooked mixture is beaten without cooling—the secret: a stick of frozen butter.

3 cups sugar
5 tablespoons cocoa
Pinch of salt
1½ cups milk
¼ pound butter, frozen
4 tablespoons peanut butter
1½ teaspoons vanilla

Combine the sugar, cocoa, and salt in a heavy 4-quart saucepan. Stir in the milk.

Place over medium-high heat; cook, stirring slowly, until the mixture comes to a boil. Turn heat to medium, stirring occasionally (slowly), to 236° to 238°, or until a small amount dropped into cold water forms a soft but slightly firm ball.

Remove from the heat and add the frozen butter and peanut butter. Stir slowly until the butter is almost melted, then add the vanilla.

Beat immediately, using an electric mixer set at medium speed, until the mixture is thickened and begins to adhere to the sides of the pan (about 5 minutes).

Pour into a buttered 9-inch layer cake pan. Let stand until completely cool, then cut into squares.

Makes about 1¾ pounds.

WHITE SATIN CHRISTMAS FUDGE

This fudge has the look of Christmas: it is snowy white and is filled with pecans and red and green candied cherries. It is a joy to make, a pleasure to give.

¼ pound butter
4 cups sugar
½ cup light corn syrup
1 cup light cream
½ cup water
1 teaspoon salt
½ cup marshmallow creme
2 teaspoons vanilla
½ cup red candied cherries, cut in quarters
½ cup green candied cherries, cut in quarters
½ cup pecan halves

Melt the butter in a heavy 4-quart saucepan over low heat. Using a rubber spatula, bring it up around the sides of the pan to grease it well.

Add the sugar, corn syrup, cream, water, and salt. Cook over low heat, stirring constantly, until the sugar is dissolved.

Continue cooking over medium heat, stirring occasionally, to 238°, or until a little of the syrup dropped into cold water forms a soft ball.

Remove from the heat and allow to cool, without disturbing, until lukewarm (110°). Blend in the marshmallow creme and vanilla. Beat until the mixture loses its gloss and starts to thicken. Quickly stir in the cherries and pecans; then spread the mixture into an even layer in a lightly buttered 9 x 12 x 2-inch pan.

Cool until firm, then cut into squares.
Makes about 9 dozen pieces.

ALMOND FUDGE ROLLS

The fudge for these rolls is cooked and beaten as for other fudge but is then kneaded to make it extra creamy. The mixture is formed into rolls, dipped into melted chocolate, and rolled in chopped almonds.

> 2 tablespoons butter
> 2 squares (2 ounces) unsweetened chocolate
> 3 cups sugar
> ¼ cup honey
> 1 cup milk
> ⅛ teaspoon salt
> 1 teaspoon vinegar
> ½ teaspoon almond extract
> 1 cup (6 ounces) semisweet chocolate morsels, melted
> 1½ cups blanched almonds, finely chopped

Lightly grease the sides of a heavy 3-quart saucepan. Add the butter and unsweetened chocolate. Cook over low heat, stirring until the two are melted and the mixture is smooth.

Add the sugar, honey, milk, and salt. Continue stirring over low heat until the sugar is dissolved. Then cover the pan; bring the mixture to a boil; cook 1 to 2 minutes, or until the steam has melted the sugar crystals down from the sides.

Remove the cover; continue cooking over medium heat without stirring to 238°, or until a little of the syrup forms a soft ball in cold water. Remove from heat; add the vinegar. Cool, without stirring, to lukewarm (110°).

Add the almond extract and beat with a wooden spoon until the mixture begins to thicken and lose its gloss. Turn out onto a buttered plate. Let stand until it is cool enough to handle. Knead a few minutes, or until very creamy.

Divide the fudge into fourths, then form each into a roll about 1½ inches in diameter. Chill until firm.

Dip the rolls into the melted chocolate, then roll in the chopped almonds to coat. Cut into ½-inch slices for serving.

Makes about 2½ pounds.

ORANGE-PECAN FUDGE SQUARES

An orange-flavored white fudge filled with pecans and currants.

> *2 cups sugar*
> *1 cup light cream*
> *Grated rind of ½ orange*
> *2 tablespoons butter*
> *¼ cup pecans, chopped*
> *¼ cup currants*

Combine the sugar, cream, and orange rind in a heavy 2-quart saucepan. Cook over medium heat, stirring constantly, to 234°, or until a little of the syrup forms a soft ball when dropped in cold water.

Remove from the heat; add the butter and, without stirring, cool to lukewarm (110°).

Beat until the mixture loses its gloss. Beat in the pecans and currants. Spread in an 8-inch square buttered pan. Cool until firm, then cut into squares.

Makes about 1 pound.

DATE-NUT ROLLS

2 cups sugar
1 cup evaporated milk
1 cup finely chopped dates
1 cup chopped walnuts
1 teaspoon vanilla
¾ cup chopped walnuts for rolling

Combine the sugar and milk in a heavy 2-quart sauce-pan. Place over medium heat and stir just until the sugar dissolves. Cover the pan; bring to a boil and cook 1 minute, or until the sugar crystals are melted down from the sides.

Remove the cover and continue cooking, stirring constantly, to 234°, or until a little of the mixture forms a soft ball when dropped in cold water.

Remove from the heat and add the dates, 1 cup of walnuts, and vanilla; mix well. Then let cool without disturbing until lukewarm (110°).

Beat until the mixture begins to thicken and lose its gloss. Turn out onto a buttered plate. Let stand until it is cool enough to handle. Then knead a few minutes until very creamy.

Divide the mixture into two parts, then form each into a roll about 1½ inches in diameter. Spread half of the remaining walnuts out on a sheet of waxed paper. Roll one log of candy in the nuts to coat, then wrap in the waxed paper and let stand until firm. Repeat with the remaining roll. For serving, cut into ½-inch slices.

Makes about 3 dozen slices.

PEANUT BUTTER FUDGE

Rich and creamy, but best of all, this fudge requires no beating. It is so delicious you'll be tempted to eat it while it's still warm. It should be chilled, however, for neater cutting.

> 2 cups sugar
> ⅔ cup milk
> 1 cup marshmallow creme
> 1 cup crunchy-style peanut butter
> 1 teaspoon vanilla

Combine the sugar and milk in a heavy 2-quart saucepan. Stir over medium heat until the mixture comes to a full boil; then continue cooking, without stirring, to 240°, or until the mixture forms a fairly firm ball when dropped into cold water.

Remove from the heat and stir in the marshmallow creme and peanut butter, then the vanilla. Continue stirring until well blended.

Pour into a lightly buttered 8-inch square pan. Chill at least 20 minutes, or until set, before cutting into 1-inch squares.

Makes 64 pieces.

OPERA CREAM FUDGE

So rich even a small piece will satisfy that sweet-tooth craving.

2 cups granulated sugar
2 cups light brown sugar (packed)
¼ teaspoon salt
2 tablespoons light corn syrup
1½ cups milk
1 cup evaporated milk (not diluted)
½ cup heavy cream
2 teaspoons vanilla
1½ cups pecans, chopped

Lightly grease the sides of a heavy 4-quart saucepan. Add the sugars, salt, corn syrup, milk, evaporated milk, and cream. Cook over low heat, stirring constantly, until the sugar is dissolved.

When the mixture comes to a boil, cook over medium heat, stirring constantly to prevent scorching, to 234°, or until a small amount of syrup dropped into cold water forms a soft ball.

Remove from the heat and cool to lukewarm (110°) without stirring.

Add the vanilla and beat until the mixture loses its gloss and is thick enough to hold a shape. Add the nuts and quickly pour out into a lightly greased 8-inch square pan. Cool until firm, then cut into squares.

Makes about 3 pounds.

OLD-FASHIONED PENUCHE

There are many variations on this theme, and several spellings of the word: Penochi, Panocha—whatever. It is a type of fudge made with brown sugar and nuts.

> *2 tablespoons butter*
> *¾ cup light cream*
> *1 cup dark brown sugar (packed)*
> *1½ cups granulated sugar*
> *1 teaspoon vanilla*
> *¾ cup walnuts, coarsely chopped*

Melt the butter in a heavy 2-quart saucepan. Swirl the butter around the sides of the pan to coat.

Add the cream. Place over low heat and bring to the boiling point. Add the sugars and stir well to dissolve.

Cover the pan and again bring to a boil over low heat; cook about 1 minute or until the sugar crystals have dissolved from the sides of the pan.

Remove the cover and continue cooking over low heat without stirring to 238°, or until a small amount of the mixture forms a soft ball in cold water.

Remove from the heat and let stand (without disturbing) until lukewarm (110°). Add the vanilla and walnuts.

Beat until creamy and the mixture starts to lose its gloss.

Pour into a buttered 8-inch square pan. Cut into squares while still slightly warm, but firm.

Makes about 2 dozen pieces.

PECAN PRALINES

1½ cups brown sugar (packed)
1½ cups granulated sugar
3 tablespoons dark corn syrup
1 cup milk
1 teaspoon vanilla
1½ cups pecans, coarsely chopped

Combine the sugars, corn syrup, and milk in a heavy 4-quart saucepan. Cook over medium heat, stirring constantly, until the mixture comes to a boil.

Turn the heat to low and continue stirring until a little of the mixture dropped in cold water forms a soft ball (234° to 236° on a candy thermometer).

Remove from the heat and let stand 10 minutes. Stir in the vanilla and beat for 2 minutes, using a wooden spoon. Add the pecans and stir until the mixture is creamy.

Drop by spoonfuls onto waxed paper to make patties about 2½ inches in diameter. (Don't attempt to make them perfectly round; they should be slightly irregular in shape.)

Note: If the mixture becomes thick, return the pan to low heat and stir to correct the consistency.

Let the pralines stand until cold and firm, then peel from the waxed paper.

Makes about 3½ dozen patties.

COCONUT PRALINES

Coconut, yes: but also made with tangy buttermilk.

2 cups sugar
1 teaspoon baking soda
Pinch of salt
1 cup buttermilk
2 tablespoons butter
2½ cups shredded coconut

Combine the sugar, baking soda, salt, and buttermilk in a 4-quart saucepan (the soda will cause the mixture to foam excessively).

Cook over high heat, stirring constantly, to 210°. Add the butter and 2 cups of the coconut.

Continue cooking and stirring over medium heat until 230°, or until a little of the mixture dropped into cold water forms a *very* soft ball.

Remove from the heat and cool 1 to 2 minutes; then beat with a spoon until the mixture looks cloudy and slightly thickened. (Do not over-beat or the pralines will not spread.)

Immediately drop teaspoonfuls onto a lightly greased cookie sheet. Before they set, top with the remaining ½ cup coconut.

Makes about 14 small pralines.

SOUR CREAM CANDY

The sour cream provides a tangy flavor; pecans and cherries give the candy color.

> 2 cups sugar
> ¾ cup sour cream
> ½ teaspoon vanilla
> ½ cup broken pecans
> 10 red candied cherries, sliced

Combine the sugar and sour cream in a heavy 2-quart saucepan. Place over low heat and stir just until the sugar dissolves. Cover the pan; bring to a boil and cook 1 minute, or until the sugar crystals are melted down from the sides.

Remove the cover and continue cooking without stirring over low heat to 235°, or until a little of the mixture forms a soft ball when dropped in cold water.

Let cool without disturbing until lukewarm (110°).

Add the vanilla, pecans, and cherries. Beat until the candy loses its gloss and is creamy.

Pour into a lightly greased 8-inch square pan. Cut into squares while still warm.

Makes about 1 pound.

DIVINITY

A time-honored confection: pure and white.

2⅓ cups sugar
⅔ cup light corn syrup
½ cup water
¼ teaspoon salt
2 egg whites
1 teaspoon vanilla

Combine the sugar, corn syrup, water, and salt in a heavy 2-quart saucepan. Stir over low heat until the sugar is dissolved.

Cover and bring to a boil; then cook 1 minute, just until the sugar crystals on the side of the pan dissolve.

Remove the cover and cook over low heat, without stirring, to 265°, or until a little of the syrup dropped into cold water forms a firm ribbon that bends when lifted from the water.

Begin beating the egg whites, using an electric mixer, when the syrup is almost cooked to the proper degree. Beat until very stiff peaks are formed, but whites are still moist.

Gradually pour the syrup in a thin, steady stream over the beaten egg whites. (Do not scrape the pan.) When the syrup has been added, add the vanilla and continue beating at high speed until the mixture loses its gloss.

Drop by teaspoonfuls onto waxed paper.

Makes about 1½ pounds.

SEAFOAM

The basic difference between Seafoam and Divinity is the type of sugar required: white vs. brown.

> *3½ cups light brown sugar (packed)*
> *1 cup water*
> *1 tablespoon vinegar*
> *2 egg whites*
> *1 teaspoon vanilla*
> *⅛ teaspoon salt*

Combine the sugar, water, and vinegar in a heavy 3-quart saucepan. Cook over low heat, stirring constantly, only until the sugar is dissolved.

Cook without stirring over low heat to 240°, or until the syrup forms a firm ball in cold water. Remove from the heat.

Begin beating the egg whites, using an electric mixer, when the syrup is almost cooked. Beat until very stiff peaks are formed, but whites are still moist.

When the syrup stops bubbling, slowly pour it into the egg whites (in a steady stream), while beating. (Do not scrape the pan.)

Add the vanilla and salt, and continue beating until the candy is thick enough to hold a shape and loses its gloss. (Test by dropping a small amount from a spoon onto waxed paper.)

Drop by teaspoonfuls onto a cookie sheet that has been covered with waxed paper.

Makes about 5 dozen pieces.

PULLED BUTTER MINTS

Although like old-fashioned taffy, this candy is creamy rather than chewy when stored a day or two to ripen.

> 4 tablespoons butter
> 1 cup hot water
> 2 cups sugar
>   Green food coloring
> ¾ teaspoon peppermint extract
>   Confectioners' sugar

Combine the butter, hot water, and sugar in a 2-quart saucepan. Place over low heat and stir until the sugar is dissolved, the butter is melted, and the mixture is boiling gently. Stir in 3 or 4 drops of green food coloring.

Cover and cook 3 minutes to wash down any sugar crystals. Then remove the cover and cook without stirring to 260°, or until a little of the syrup forms a hard ball in cold water.

Remove from the heat and carefully pour the hot syrup onto a well-greased large platter set on a cooling rack. (Hold the saucepan close to the platter to prevent splattering; do not scrape out the last of the syrup.) Sprinkle the peppermint extract on the top; do not stir. Let stand without disturbing until the mixture is cool enough to handle.

Knead the candy until it can be picked up for pulling. Then pull, folding it back on itself until it is very firm and loses most of its gloss.

Stretch into a rope about ½ inch in diameter and cut with scissors into one-inch lengths. As they are cut, drop them into a pan of confectioners' sugar to prevent sticking.

Layer the candy with the sugar in a wide-mouth quart jar. Screw on the lid and let stand at room temperature until creamy (this may take a few hours or up to 2 days).

Then place in a strainer and shake off the excess sugar. Return to the jar for storing.

Makes about ¾ pound.

FRENCH CHOCOLATE TRUFFLES

A classic French sweet, often served in tiny fluted paper cups.

> ½ *pound sweet butter*
> ½ *pound (8 squares) semisweet chocolate*
> ½ *cup brandy*
> *Cocoa*

Cut the butter into pieces directly into a heavy saucepan. Melt over medium-low heat; then turn heat to medium, and when the butter bubbles, stir to mix well. When the bubbling turns to foam, remove from the heat.

Let stand 5 minutes to settle, then skim any remaining foam from the top. Carefully pour off the clear liquid, leaving the light-brown sediment in the saucepan.

Return the butter (this is called clarified butter) to a clean saucepan. Add the chocolate. Stir over very low heat until the chocolate is melted and smooth. Remove from the heat and cool slightly. Stir in the brandy. Chill until the mixture is firm enough to handle, several hours or overnight.

Note: If the butter rises to the top as the mixture chills, it can easily be blended in before it becomes solid.

Shape the chilled mixture into balls about 1 inch in diameter and roll in cocoa to coat. Place on a plate and refrigerate until firm. Then store in a tightly covered container in the refrigerator. Will keep well for several weeks.

Makes 3 to 3½ dozen truffles.

CHEWY AND CHARD CANDIES

This collection of old-time recipes includes an array of delights: soft gelatin candy, chewy caramels and nougat, crunchy brittles and smooth hard candy.

Here you will find Turkish Delight: the forerunner of gumdrops; Nougat; Salt Water Taffy, said to have originated in Atlantic City; porous easy-to-eat Peanut Brittle; and English Toffee, a crunchy specialty coated with chocolate and almonds.

TURKISH DELIGHTS

3 envelopes unflavored gelatin
½ cup cold water
2 cups sugar
⅛ teaspoon salt
½ cup hot water
    Grated rind and juice (¼ cup) of 1 orange
    Juice of 1 lemon (2 tablespoons)
    Red food coloring
    Confectioners' sugar

Soften the gelatin in the cold water.

Combine the sugar, salt and hot water in a saucepan; heat to boiling, stirring constantly. Stir in the softened gelatin; turn the heat down and simmer, without stirring, for 20 minutes.

Remove from the heat and stir in the grated rind, orange and lemon juice, and a little red food coloring to tint the mixture a bright red (¼ teaspoon is about right). Let stand 3 minutes.

Strain the mixture into a 8 x 4-inch loaf pan which has been rinsed with cold water. Let stand without disturbing until slightly jellied (to prevent filming the sides of the pan); then refrigerate overnight.

Loosen around the sides of the pan with a wet spatula. Slip the spatula down one end and underneath the jellied mixture, then pull it out of the pan with your hands. (It is firm and pliable, and easily handled.)

Cut into 1-inch squares. (Use a large, sharp knife and press the blade down through the gelatin, rather than drawing the knife through it.) Roll in confectioners' sugar to coat.

Store in one layer in a tightly covered container at room temperature. The candies will stay moist for about 2 weeks.

Makes 32 pieces.

SALT WATER TAFFY

Salt water taffy is thought to have originated in Atlantic City, where salty seawater was used in its making. It is a light-colored taffy, delicately flavored, in contrast to what is considered old-fashioned taffy, which is made with molasses.

> 1 cup sugar
> 2 tablespoons cornstarch
> ¾ cup light corn syrup
> ½ cup water
> ½ teaspoon salt
> 2 tablespoons butter
> 2 teaspoons vanilla

Combine the sugar and cornstarch in a heavy 2-quart saucepan. Stir in the corn syrup, water, salt, and butter.

Cook over medium heat, stirring constantly, until the mixture boils and the sugar is dissolved.

Continue cooking without stirring to 256° to 260°, or until a little of the syrup dropped in cold water forms a hard ball. Remove from the heat.

Note: The lower temperatures will result in a soft, chewy taffy; the higher degrees will produce a firmer one.

Pour out onto a well-greased platter or baking sheet with sides, holding the saucepan close to the sheet so that it does not splatter. (Do not scrape the pan or spread the syrup.)

Let stand until cool enough so that the syrup holds a finger imprint. Then sprinkle the vanilla over the top. Using a buttered spatula, fold the edges over toward the center; continue this process until the mixture can be gathered into a ball.

With lightly buttered hands, pull the taffy, folding it back on itself and stretching until it turns white and has a satinlike finish.

Stretch the pulled taffy into a long rope, about ¾-inch in diameter (or slightly less). Then cut with kitchen scissors into 1-inch pieces.

Wrap individually in squares of waxed paper, twisting the ends.

Makes about 1 pound.

NOUGAT

This chewy candy is named after the French town of Nougat where it originated. It is made with almonds and pistachios.

2 cups sugar
1½ cups light corn syrup
¼ cup water
¼ teaspoon salt
2 egg whites
4 tablespoons soft butter
1 teaspoon vanilla
¾ cup blanched and toasted almonds, chopped
¼ cup blanched pistachios, chopped

Combine the sugar, corn syrup, water, and salt in a heavy 3-quart saucepan. Cook, stirring over low heat, until the sugar is dissolved. Then cook over medium heat without stirring to 250°, or until a small amount of the syrup forms a hard ball in cold water. (During the cooking, brush down any sugar crystals with a pastry brush dipped in warm water.)

Just before the syrup is cooked, beat the egg whites (use an electric mixer) until stiff but not dry. Gradually beat in about one-fourth (not more) of the hot syrup; continue beating until the mixture holds its shape.

Brush the sides of the pan again to dissolve the hardened syrup which was formed during pouring; then cook the remaining syrup to 300°, or until a little of the syrup forms hard, brittle threads in cold water. (Cook slowly the last 20° to prevent the syrup from scorching.)

Pour the hot syrup in a slow, steady stream over the

egg white mixture while beating. When the mixture begins to hold a shape, add the butter and vanilla. Continue beating until thick and satiny. (Test by dipping out a spoonful of the mixture; when slightly cooled it should not stick to your finger when touched.) Stir in the almonds and pistachios.

Turn into a well-buttered 8-inch square pan; press evenly. Grease the top, using lightly buttered fingers. Let stand overnight. It must be very firm for cutting.

Turn the nougat out in a block, then cut into 1 x 1½-inch oblongs. Wrap each piece separately in waxed paper. Store in a tightly covered container in a cool dry place.

Note: For best flavor let stand a few days before serving. It will keep well for at least 1 month.

Makes about 1½ pounds.

CREAM CARAMELS

Chewy, chewy caramels made with heavy cream and flavored with vanilla.

> 2 cups heavy cream
> 1 cup milk
> 2 cups sugar
> 1½ cups light corn syrup
> 1 teaspoon vanilla

Combine the cream and milk in a measuring cup. Then pour 1½ cups of the mixture into a heavy 4-quart saucepan. Stir in the sugar and corn syrup. Cook over medium heat, stirring constantly, until the mixture comes to a boil.

Continue cooking, stirring occasionally, to 234°, or until a small amount of the mixture forms a soft ball in cold water.

Slowly add the remaining 1½ cups cream mixture, so that the mixture continues to boil. Continue cooking, stirring occasionally to keep from scorching, to 244° or until a little of the syrup forms a firm ball in cold water.

Remove from the heat and stir in the vanilla. Pour into a lightly buttered 9-inch square pan. Cool completely.

Turn the block of candy out onto a smooth surface. Cut into small squares with a large sharp knife. Wrap each piece in waxed paper.

Makes 2¼ pounds.

ENGLISH TOFFEE

Crunchy candy coated with chocolate and topped with almonds.

½ *pound butter*
1 ⅓ *cups light brown sugar (packed)*
⅔ *cup toasted blanched almonds,*
   coarsely chopped
3 *bars (⅞ to 1 ounce) milk chocolate*
½ *cup toasted blanched almonds, coarsely*
   chopped (for topping)

Combine the butter and sugar in a heavy 2-quart saucepan. Place over low heat and stir constantly until the mixture comes to a boil.

Continue cooking, stirring occasionally, until a small amount dropped in cold water is brittle (290° on a candy thermometer).

Add ⅔ cup coarsely chopped almonds. (Avoid over-stirring as this will cause sugaring.) Immediately pour into a well-greased 13 x 9-inch pan. Let stand until the mixture is set but still warm.

Arrange the chocolate bars on top of the warm toffee. (Break into squares for easier spreading.) As the chocolate softens, spread with a spatula. Sprinkle with the remaining chopped almonds. (These should be chopped slightly finer than those used in the toffee mixture so that they will adhere as the chocolate firms.) Press in lightly. Cool thoroughly, then break into irregular pieces.

Makes about 1⅓ pounds toffee.

OLD-TIME PEANUT BRITTLE

A light-textured brittle that is easy to eat. The recipe makes a large amount.

> 2 cups sugar
> 1 cup light corn syrup
> 1 cup water
> ¼ pound butter
> 1 pound (about 3¼ cups) unsalted raw peanuts*
> ½ teaspoon salt
> 1 teaspoon hot water
> 1 teaspoon vanilla
> 1½ teaspoons baking soda (free of lumps)

* Raw peanuts can be purchased in a health food store.

Combine the sugar, corn syrup, water, and butter in a heavy 4- to 5-quart saucepan. Cook over medium heat, stirring until the sugar is dissolved. Then continue cooking without stirring to 230°–234°, or until the syrup spins a 2-inch thread when dropped from a spoon. Gradually stir in the peanuts so that the mixture continues to boil. Turn the heat to low and cook, stirring constantly, to 280°.

Remove from heat and stir in the salt, hot water, and vanilla. Return to medium heat (to give a good golden color) and continue stirring to 300°, or to the hard-crack stage.

Remove from the heat, add the baking soda, and stir just until the mixture foams up well (no longer or it may sugar).

Immediately pour out onto a greased 15 x 10-inch

pan. Spread out as thinly as possible with a greased spatula.

Cool, then break into pieces. Store in an airtight container.

Makes about 2¼ pounds.

ROYAL BRITTLE

An elegant brittle made with walnuts and almonds.

> 1 cup granulated sugar
> ½ cup light brown sugar (packed)
> ¼ cup light corn syrup
> 1 teaspoon cider vinegar
> ⅓ cup water
> ⅛ teaspoon salt
> pinch baking soda
> 2 tablespoons butter
> ¾ cup combined broken walnuts and almond halves

Combine the sugars, corn syrup, vinegar, and water in a heavy 2-quart saucepan. Cook over low heat, stirring until the sugar is dissolved.

Continue to cook, without stirring, to 300°, or the hard-crack stage. (During the cooking, wash down the sugar crystals from the sides of the pan with a pastry brush dipped in hot water.)

Remove from the heat. Add the salt, baking soda, butter, and nuts. Stir only enough to mix. Turn out onto a buttered cookie sheet (do not scrape the pan). Spread thinly with a buttered spatula.

Loosen the candy while still warm. Break into irregular pieces.

Makes about 1 pound.

BUTTERSCOTCH

A hard rather than soft butterscotch that keeps well.

2 cups sugar
⅔ cup dark corn syrup
¼ cup heavy cream
¼ cup water
4 tablespoons butter

Combine the sugar, corn syrup, cream, and water in a heavy 3-quart saucepan. Cook over medium heat, stirring constantly, until the mixture comes to a boil. Continue cooking, stirring occasionally, to 260°, or until a little of the mixture dropped into very cold water forms a ball which is hard enough to hold its shape.

Add the butter a tablespoon at a time. Continue cooking, stirring constantly, to 280°, or until a small amount of the mixture dropped into very cold water separates into threads which are hard but not brittle.

Pour out into well-buttered 8 x 8 x 2-inch pan. (Do not scrape the pan.)

Let stand until a light film appears on top of the candy, about 10 minutes. Then, using a wide spatula, mark the candy into small squares. (Just press the spatula lightly onto the top; do not attempt to cut through.) Keep pressing along the marks so that the candy forms rounded puffs which hold a shape; then cut completely through.

Cool thoroughly, then turn out. (A sharp rap on the pan on a table will release the candy.) Break apart any candies that stick together.

Makes 1¼ pounds.

FRUIT AND NUT CONFECTIONS

Most of these confections have fruits or nuts as their bases. Although some require long cooking time, others are made quickly and easily.

Here are chewy Candied Orange Peel; chocolate Peanut Bark; fanciful Sugarplums—dried fruits stuffed with a creamy uncooked fondant; and Pink Popcorn Cake, a special treat for children.

CANDIED ORANGE PEEL

Strips of pleasantly bitter peel coated with sugar.

> 6 seedless oranges
> 2 quarts warm water
> 2 tablespoons salt
> 2 cups sugar
> 2 tablespoons honey
> 1 cup water
> 1 envelope unflavored gelatin softened
>   in 2 tablespoons water
> Granulated sugar for rolling

Cut the oranges in half; squeeze to extract the juice. (The juice is not required in this recipe.)

Combine the warm water and salt in a large bowl; add the orange peel, weight down with a plate, and let stand overnight.

Drain the peel. Place in a heavy saucepan and cover with water. Bring to a boil, then drain. Repeat this process three times. (This will take away some of the bitterness.) Do not drain the peel during the last process; cook slowly for 30 minutes, or until tender. Remove from heat and drain.

Scrape the inner surface of the rinds with a teaspoon to remove the soft pulp, leaving the white spongy coating. Then cut the peel into ⅛- to ¼-inch strips (with scissors), making them as long and uniform as possible.

Combine the sugar, honey, and 1 cup water in a large, heavy saucepan. Bring to a boil, stirring; then add the strips of peel. Cook over low heat until transparent and most of the syrup has been absorbed, about 40 minutes. (Watch carefully toward the end to prevent scorching.)

Remove from heat and add the softened gelatin. Stir until dissolved, then pour the contents into a colander to drain off the excess syrup.

One by one, remove the strips to a sheet of waxed paper that has been coated with granulated sugar. Roll them in the sugar, then place on a separate sheet of waxed paper to dry slightly and stiffen. (This may take a day.)

Store in a tightly covered container. The peel will keep well for weeks.

Makes about 1¾ pounds.

Note: Four medium-size grapefruit may be substituted for the oranges.

SUGARPLUMS

Colorful sugarplums by the dozens made from a single batch of fondant, a variety of dried fruits, nuts, and garnishes. The delicious fondant is quickly and easily prepared without cooking.

1 pound confectioners' sugar
¼ pound cold butter
2 tablespoons heavy cream
1 teaspoon vanilla or ½ teaspoon almond extract
Pitted ready-to-eat prunes
Candied cherries
Pitted dates
Walnut or pecan halves
Granulated sugar for rolling
Candied cherries and silver dragees
for garnish

Pour the unsifted confectioners' sugar into a large bowl. Cut the butter from the stick into small slivers, dropping them into the sugar. Add the cream and vanilla or almond extract. Work with your fingertips until the mixture clings together somewhat.

Turn the mixture onto a sheet of waxed paper. Knead by pushing the mixture against the surface with the heel of your hand, lifting the edges of the waxed paper to add and incorporate any crumbs of dough. Continue kneading in this manner until the mixture is well blended, smooth, and creamy. Wrap in the waxed paper and chill just long enough so that the fondant can be handled easily without sticking.

Prunes: Slit the tops of the prunes and spread slightly. Roll a small portion of the chilled fondant into a ball and press into the cavity. Garnish with a sliver of candied cherry.

Cherries: Cut a cross in the top of each cherry; spread slightly to form petals. Fill with a small ball of fondant and decorate the tops with a few silver dragees.

Dates: Cut the dates partway through and press a small portion of the fondant into the cavities. Roll the filled dates in granulated sugar.

Walnuts or Pecans: Shape the fondant into small balls; place between two walnut or pecan halves; press together lightly.

Store in one layer in a tightly covered container in the refrigerator. The sugarplums will keep well up to 2 weeks.

Note: When the desired number of sugarplums have been made, divide the remaining fondant into small portions. Add a few drops of desired food coloring and knead again until the color is even. Chill if necessary, then form into small balls about ¾ inch in diameter. Form into almond shapes and press a toasted blanched almond into the top of each.

APRICOT STRAWS

An easily made confection.

½ pound dried apricots
Hot water
½ cup granulated sugar

Place the apricots in the top of a double boiler. Add hot water from the tap to cover; let stand 5 minutes. Drain off the water.

Set the pan over boiling water, cover and steam the apricots 5 minutes.

Spread out onto a large sheet of waxed paper, skin-side up. Flatten each apricot with the palm of your hand. Cut into ⅛-inch strips with scissors. Roll in the sugar to coat.

Set aside on a separate sheet of waxed paper in a cool place until the straws dry somewhat and become stiff. (This may take a day.)

Store in a tightly covered container in a cool place. *Makes about ¾ pound.*

CREAMED WALNUTS

Walnuts with a sour-cream candy coating.

1½ cups sugar
½ cup sour cream
1½ teaspoons vanilla
2 cups walnut halves

Combine the sugar and sour cream in a 2-quart saucepan. Cook, stirring, over medium heat until the sugar is dissolved. Continue cooking without stirring to 240°, or until the mixture forms a firm soft ball in water.

Remove from the heat; add the vanilla and walnuts. Stir immediately until just slightly thickened and the mixture looks cloudy. (Do not over-stir or the mixture will not spread.)

Turn out onto waxed paper and separate the walnuts, using two forks.

ROCKY ROADS

A popular candy because of its simplicity. This version is made with chunky peanut butter—a variation of the original concept which is made with broken nuts and cut marshmallows.

15 large marshmallows
1 cup crunchy-style peanut butter
2 cups (12 ounces) semisweet chocolate morsels

Cut the marshmallows into quarters, using wet kitchen scissors. Arrange on the bottom of a buttered 8-inch square pan.

Melt the peanut butter and chocolate morsels in a saucepan over very low heat. Stir to blend as the mixture begins to melt. When completely melted and blended, dribble over the top of the marshmallows. Spread evenly.

Chill until firm, then cut into squares.

Makes 36 squares.

CLUSTERS

Another quickly made chocolate confection, with peanuts and raisins.

1 cup (6 ounces) semisweet chocolate morsels
¼ cup light corn syrup
1 tablespoon water
1 cup raisins
1 cup salted peanuts

Combine the chocolate morsels, corn syrup, and water in the top of a double boiler; melt over hot (not boiling) water. Remove from heat and stir in the raisins and peanuts.

Drop by teaspoonfuls on a lightly greased cookie sheet. Cool until firm.

Makes about 3 dozen.

PEANUT BARK

So simple, it's hardly a recipe.

1 cup (6 ounces) semisweet chocolate morsels
5 tablespoons warm evaporated milk (undiluted)
1 cup salted peanuts

Melt the chocolate over hot (not boiling) water; stir until smooth.

Remove from the heat and immediately stir in the milk and peanuts until blended.

Pour the mixture onto waxed paper and flatten with a spatula. Let stand until firm, then break into irregular pieces.

Makes about 2½ dozen.

BOURBON BALLS

Traditionally served at Christmastime in Kentucky—
the state famous for its bourbon whiskey.

> *1½ cups finely crushed vanilla wafers*
> *1 cup sifted confectioners' sugar*
> *3 tablespoons cocoa*
> *1 cup finely chopped pecans*
> *3 tablespoons white corn syrup*
> *¼ cup bourbon*
>   *Confectioners' sugar for coating*

Combine the crushed wafers, confectioners' sugar, cocoa, and pecans in a mixing bowl. Add the corn syrup and bourbon; blend well.

Form into 1-inch balls. Then roll in confectioners' sugar to coat. Place on waxed paper and allow to dry for several hours.

Store in an airtight container for several days before serving. The flavor improves with aging.

Makes about 3 dozen balls.

PINK POPCORN CAKE

Instead of being formed into balls, pink glazed pop-corn is pressed into an angelfood cake pan to shape. A special treat for the children.

> 2 cups sugar
> ¾ cup water
> 3 tablespoons white vinegar
> Red food coloring
> 4½ quarts freshly popped corn

Combine the sugar, water, and vinegar in a heavy 2-quart saucepan. Cook over low heat, stirring just until the sugar is dissolved. Continue cooking to 230–234°, or until the syrup spins a 2-inch thread when dropped from a spoon. Remove from heat and stir in a few drops of red food coloring to obtain a pink shade (10 drops is about right).

Pour the syrup in a thin stream over the popped corn, using a spoon to mix well and cover each kernel. The syrup will distribute evenly if the popcorn is warm. (Keep it warm by heating in a 250° oven while the syrup is cooking.) While the mixture is still warm, press it into a greased 9-inch angelfood cake pan. Cool and invert after removing from the pan.

To serve, pull off pieces or cut into wedges.

Makes one 9-inch cake.

INDEX